Eloi Rylan Koios (Ed.)

Security Service Federal Credit Union

Eloi Rylan Koios (Ed.)

Security Service Federal Credit Union

Credit Union, San Antonio

Tract

Imprint

Publisher:
Tract is a trademark of
International Book Market Service Ltd., 17 Rue Meldrum, Beau Bassin, 1713-01 Mauritius
Email: info@bookmarketservice.com
Website: www.bookmarketservice.com

Published in 2011

Printed in: U.S.A., U.K., Germany. This book was not produced in Mauritius.

ISBN: 978-613-7-92159-3

Contents

Articles

References

Security Service Federal Credit Union

Type	Credit union
Industry	Financial services
Founded	1956
Headquarters	San Antonio, Texas, USA
Number of locations	69 (36 service centers in Texas; 19 in Colorado; 14 in Utah (2011)
Area served	South Texas, Limited areas in Colorado, Utah
Key people	Bob Egger (Chairman)[1] David Reynolds (President)
Services	Savings; Checking; Consumer Loans; Mortgages; Credit cards; Investments
Employees	1,368 full-time; 184 part-time[2]
Subsidiaries	SSFCU CUSO [3] CU Direct Corporation [4] CU Cooperative Systems CU Service Network of Colorado[2] Norbel CU [5]
Website	http://www.ssfcu.org/

Security Service Federal Credit Union, commonly shortened to **SSFCU**, is a federally insured, state chartered, 6 billion dollar, more than 840,000 members, natural person, credit union operating from over 65 service centers in Texas, Colorado, and Utah. Security Service is the largest credit union in San Antonio, Texas, 3rd largest in Colorado, and the 8th largest in the United States, with access to +4,000 credit union locations nationwide through CU Service Centers shared branching.[6]

The routing number for Security Service Federal Credit Union is 314088637.[7]

History

Security Service Federal Credit Union began in 1956 with eight members and $25 in deposits. This not-for-profit, member-owned financial institution was founded to serve the financial needs of the U.S. Air Force Security Service. The credit union charter has expanded to serve more than 840,000 members and more than 2,100 ways to join including several geographic locations.

Mergers and acquisitions

Mergers, initiated by other credit unions, and some facilitated by the National Credit Union Administration, have helped expand the SSFCU field of membership and also responsible for the credit union entry into Colorado and Utah. A merger with the Fort Carson Federal Credit Union in 1980 brought Security Service to Colorado Springs and Pueblo, CO, with the merger of Mt. Carmel Credit Union in 1989. In 2004, SSFCU acquired Diakonia Credit Union in Denver, Colorado which added their presence in the Denver market. In 2007, Security Service acquired New Horizons Community Credit Union in Denver, Colorado, further expanding the Denver area with 4 new service centers, and Diocese of Corpus Christi Credit Union in Corpus Christi, Texas, establishing a service center in the Coastal Bend area of Texas. Also in 2007, SSFCU merged with Kilowatt Federal Credit Union in Harlingen, Texas, with 2 service centers in the Rio Grande Valley. In 2008, SSFCU merged with Horizon Credit Union in Portland, Texas (adding 3 additional Coastal bend locations) and Bexar County Teacher's Federal Credit Union in San Antonio, Texas (their first location in the downtown area of San Antonio). 2009 brought the credit union with two more acquisitions, another credit union in the Denver area (Aurora Catholic Credit Union) and its first presence known in West Texas ironically called West Texas Credit Union in El Paso, TX.[8] During the late 2000s recession, SSFCU acquired the failed Norbel Credit Union of Colorado and its 16,000 members in a liquidation process. The Norbel board of directors selected Security Service to be its acquirer judging it to be extremely well suited to serve its members.[9] In December 2010, the NCUA approved Security Service's offer to assume Salt Lake City's Beehive Credit Union's assets, making its first presence in the cities of Salt Lake City, Provo, Riverton, Sandy, South Jordan and St. George, Utah.[10] In February 2011, Security Service FCU also acquired Family First Federal Credit Union of Orem, Utah. In addition to Orem, Security Service added locations in Pleasant Grove, Springville, American Fork, Payson and Lindon, Utah to its network of service centers.[11]

May 1974	San Antonio Air Guard CU	San Antonio, TX
April 1975	Camp Stanley CU	Uvalde, TX
March 1980	Ft. Carson FCU	Ft. Carson, CO
April 1983	Honey Capital CU	Uvalde, TX
September 1986	Southwest Methodist FCU	San Antonio, TX
July 1987	Metrotech CU	San Antonio, TX
October 1987	Joske's FCU	San Antonio, TX
February 1989	Mt. Carmel CU (Catholic)	Pueblo, CO
March 1989	Bordens Dairy CU	San Antonio, TX
February 1993	San Antonio Light Credit Union	San Antonio, TX
September 2004	Diakonia CU	Denver, CO
July 2007	Diocese of Corpus Christi FCU	Corpus Christi, TX
	New Horizon Community CU	Denver, CO
August 2007	Kilowatt FCU	Harlingen, TX
January 2008	Horizon FCU	Portland, TX
December 2008	Bexar County Teachers FCU	San Antonio, TX
March 2009	Aurora Catholic FCU	Aurora, CO
October 2009	West Texas Credit Union	El Paso, TX
July 2010	Norbel Credit Union	Fort Collins, CO
December 2010	Beehive Credit Union	Salt Lake City, UT
February 2011	Family First Federal Credit Union	Orem, UT

Membership

A wide range of military, government, school, religious, and business organizations are Select Employee Groups (SEGs) eligible for SSFCU membership. Additionally, persons who live, work, or worship in the following communities qualify:[12]

Texas communities

- Atascosa County, Texas
- Boerne, Texas
- Cameron County, Texas
- Corpus Christi, Texas
- Hidalgo County, Texas
- Inside Loop 410
- Medina County, Texas
- South Bexar County, Texas
- Uvalde County, Texas

Colorado communities

- Southern El Paso County, Colorado
- Pueblo County, Colorado
- Denver County, Colorado
- Employees & contractors at Fort Carson, and various other SEGs

Family members of current members are also welcome to join.

Services

Security Service Federal Credit Union offers these services:

- Checking Accounts and related, including debit cards
- Savings Accounts
- Certificates of Deposit
- IRAs
- Consumer loans of all kinds
  - Lines of credit (LOC)
  - Credit cards
  - Auto loans: Car loans, motorcycle loans, etc.
  - Home equity loans and Home equity lines of credit
- Mortgages
- Federally Insured Student loans
- Direct Deposit
- Home banking

References

[1] Security Service Federal Credit Union (March 2007). "SSFCU Announces 2007-2008 Board of Directors" (http://www.ssfcu.org/corporate/news/pressreleases.aspx). . Retrieved 2008-02-04.
[2] "NCUA Form 5300 (Statement of Financial Condition)" (http://www.ibanknet.com/scripts/callreports/getbank.aspx?ibnid=usa_666581). May 2011. . Retrieved 2011.
[3] http://www.cusource.com/
[4] http://www.cudirect.com/
[5] http://www.norbel.org
[6] Facts About Security Service (https://www.ssfcu.org/en-us/about/securityservice/Pages/securityservice.aspx)
[7] Routing number (https://www.ssfcu.org/en-us/contact/Pages/routingnumber.aspx)
[8] Antonio, San (2009-10-01). "Security Service buys El Paso credit union" (http://sanantonio.bizjournals.com/sanantonio/stories/2009/09/28/daily37.html?ed=2009-10-02&ana=e_du_pub#). .
[9] Norbel closes and assets sold (http://www.coloradoan.com/article/20100730/BUSINESS/7300330/Norbel-closes-assets-sold)
[10] . http://www.ncua.gov/news/press_releases/2010/MR10-1214BeehiveCUClosesFINAL.pdf.
[11] Security Service FCU Acquires Family First Federal Credit Union (https://www.ssfcu.org/en-us/about/news/Pages/familyfirstfcu.aspx?src=familyfirst)
[12] Membership qualifications (https://www.ssfcu.org/en-us/services/join/Pages/waystojoinco.aspx)

External links

- Security Service Credit Union (http://www.ssfcu.org/) — official site
- Security Service Federal Credit Union statistics (http://www.creditunionondb.com/view/San_Antonio_TX/Security-Service-Federal-Credit-Union/11065.html)

Natural person

Variously, in jurisprudence, a **natural person** is a human being, as opposed to an artificial, legal or juristic person, i.e., an organization that the law treats for some purposes as if it were a person distinct from its members or owner. Sometimes the legal situation limits the term by limits on age, psychiatric, medical, nationality attributes, gender, sexual orientation, criminal record, official paperwork, and computer records (which may or may not be accurate).

For example, such legal provisions as Amendment XIX to the United States Constitution, which states a person can not be denied the right to vote based on gender, or Section 15 of the Canadian Charter of Rights and Freedoms, which guarantees equality rights, apply to natural persons only. In many cases fundamental human rights are implicitly granted only to natural persons; for example a corporation cannot hold public office, but it can file a lawsuit.

Credit union

A **credit union** is a cooperative financial institution that is owned and controlled by its members and operated for the purpose of promoting thrift, providing credit at competitive rates, and providing other financial services to its members.[1] [2] [3] Many credit unions exist to further community development[4] or sustainable international development on a local level.[5]

Worldwide, credit union systems vary significantly in terms of total system assets and average institution asset size,[6] ranging from volunteer operations with a handful of members to institutions with several billion dollars in assets and hundreds of thousands of members. Credit unions are typically smaller than banks; for example, the average U.S. credit union has $93 million in assets, while the average U.S. bank has $1.53 billion, as of 2007.[7]

The World Council of Credit Unions (WOCCU) defines credit unions as "not-for-profit cooperative institutions".[8] In practice however, legal arrangements vary by jurisdiction. For example in Canada credit unions are regulated as for-profit institutions, and view their mandate as earning a reasonable profit to enhance services to members and ensure stable growth.[9]

This difference in viewpoints reflects credit unions' unusual organizational structure, which attempts to solve the principal-agent problem by ensuring that the owners and the users of the institution are the same people. In any case, credit unions generally cannot accept donations and must be able to prosper in a competitive market economy.

Other names

In some places, credit unions are called by other names; for example, in many African countries they are called "savings and credit cooperative organizations" (SACCOs), "to emphasize savings before credit."[8] In Spanish-speaking countries, they are often called *cooperativas de ahorro y crédito*,[10] [11] but in Mexico they are typically called a *caja popular*.[12] French terms for "credit union" include *caisse populaire*[13] and *banque populaire*.[14] Afghan credit unions are called "Islamic investment and finance cooperatives" (IIFCs) and comply with Islamic banking practices.[8]

Differences from other financial institutions

Credit unions differ from banks and other financial institutions in that the members who have accounts in the credit union are the owners of the credit union[15] and they elect their board of directors in a democratic one-person-one-vote system regardless of the amount of money invested in the credit union.[16]

A credit union's policies governing interest rates and other matters are set by a volunteer Board of Directors elected by and from the membership itself.[17] Credit unions offer many of the same financial services as banks, often using a different terminology; common services include: share accounts (savings accounts), share draft accounts (checking accounts), credit cards, share term certificates (certificates of deposit), and online banking.[2]

Normally, only a member of a credit union may deposit money with the credit union, or borrow money from it.[2] As such, credit unions have historically marketed themselves as providing superior member service and being committed to helping members improve their financial health. In the microfinance context, "[c]redit unions provide a broader range of loan and savings products at a much cheaper cost [to their members] than do most microfinance institutions".[18]

Global dispersion

The directors of the Mulukanoor Women's Thrift Cooperative stand at the entrance to their credit union in Karimnagar district, Andhra Pradesh, India

Based on data from the World Council of Credit Unions, at the end of 2006 there were 46,377 credit unions in 97 countries around the world. Collectively they served 172 million retail members and oversaw US $1.1 trillion in assets.[19] Note that the World Council does not include data from co-operative banks, so that, for example, some nations generally seen as the pioneers of credit unionism, such as Germany, France, Netherlands and Italy, are not included in their data. The European Association of Co-operative Banks reported 34 million members in those four countries at the end of 2005.[20]

The nations with the most credit union activity are highly diverse. According to the World Council, nations with the greatest number of credit union members included the United States (87 million), India (20 million), Canada (11 million), South Korea (4.7 million), Japan (3.6 million), Mexico (3.6 million), Australia (3.5 million), Kenya (3.3 million), Ireland (3.0 million), Thailand and Brazil (2.6 million each).

Countries with the highest percentage of members in the economically active population were Dominica (147% [numbers higher than 100% are possible because the average person is a member of more than one credit union]), Ireland (110%), Barbados (72%), Trinidad & Tobago (57%), Canada (48%), the United States (43%), Benin (27%), Australia (26%), Senegal and Mali (19% each).

History

Friedrich Wilhelm Raiffeisen started credit unions in rural Germany.

Modern credit union history dates to 1852, when Franz Hermann Schulze-Delitzsch consolidated the learning from two pilot projects, one in Eilenburg and the other in Delitzsch in Germany into what are generally recognized as the first credit unions in the world. He went on to develop a highly successful urban credit union system.[21]

In 1864 Friedrich Wilhelm Raiffeisen founded the first rural credit union in Heddesdorf (now part of Neuwied) in Germany.[22] Although Schulze-Delitzsch can claim chronological precedence, Raiffeisen is often viewed as more important today. Rural communities in Germany faced a far more severe shortage of financial institutions than the cities. They were viewed as unbankable because of very small, seasonal flows of cash and very limited human resources. The organizational methods Raiffeisen refined there, which levered what is today called social capital, have become a hallmark of the global credit union identity.

By the time of Raiffeisen's death in 1888, credit unions had spread to Italy, France, the Netherlands, England and Austria, among other nations. The Raiffeisen name is still used by Raiffeisenbank, the largest banking group in Austria (with subsidiaries throughout Central and Eastern Europe), Rabobank (Netherlands) and similarly named agricultural credit unions in Germany.

The first credit union in North America, the Caisse Populaire de Lévis in Quebec, Canada, began operations on January 23, 1901 with a ten cent deposit. Founder Alphonse Desjardins, a reporter in the Canadian parliament, was moved to take up his mission in 1897 when he learned of a Montrealer who had been ordered by the court to pay nearly $5,000 in interest on a loan of $150 from a moneylender. Drawing extensively on European precedents, Desjardins developed a unique parish-based model for Quebec: the *caisse populaire*.

In the United States, St. Mary's Bank Credit Union of Manchester, New Hampshire holds the distinction as the first credit union. Assisted by a personal visit from Desjardins, St. Mary's was founded by French-speaking immigrants to Manchester from Quebec on November 24, 1908. America's Credit Union Museum now occupies the location of the home from which St. Mary's Bank Credit Union first operated.

Pierre Jay, then-Massachusetts Commissioner of Banks, and Edward Filene, a Bostonian merchant, were central in establishing enabling legislation in Massachusetts in 1909. The Woman's Educational and Industrial Union, credited with many social service initiatives, heard of this cooperative financial model and wrote to DesJardins. He provided them with the data they needed, and on November 23, 1910, they created Industrial Credit Union, the first non-faith-based or community credit union, established for all people in the greater Boston community. St. Mary's Credit Union (not to be confused with St. Mary's Bank Credit Union) was established in Marlborough in 1913. Serving any resident of the Commonwealth of Massachusetts, St. Mary's Credit Union is the oldest state-wide Credit Union nationally.[23]

Filene also created the Credit Union National Extension Bureau, the forerunner of the Credit Union National Association, which was formed as a confederation of state leagues at a meeting in Estes Park, Colorado, in 1934. Attendees at the meeting included Dora Maxwell who would go on to help establish hundreds of credit unions and programs for the poor and Louise McCarren Herring, whose work to form credit unions and ensure their safe operation earned the title of "Mother of Credit Unions" in the United States.

In the same year, Congress passed the Federal Credit Union Act, which permitted credit unions to be organized anywhere in the United States. The legislation allowed credit unions to incorporate under either state or federal law, a system of dual chartering that persists today.

Not-for-profit status and the need for a surplus

In the credit union context, "not-for-profit" should not be confused with "non-profit" charities or similar organizations.[24] Credit unions are "not-for-profit" because they operate to serve their members rather than to maximize profits.[25] [26] [27] But unlike non-profit organizations, credit unions do not rely on donations, and are financial institutions that must turn what is, in economic terms, a small profit (i.e. "surplus") to be able to continue to serve their members.[28] [29] According to WOCCU, a credit union's revenues (from loans and investments) need to exceed its operating expenses and dividends (interest paid on deposits) in order to maintain capital and solvency[30] and "credit unions use excess earnings to offer members more affordable loans, a higher return on savings, lower fees or new products and services".[8]

WOCCU's position is deeply rooted in global credit union history. F.W. Raiffeisen, the founder of the global movement, wrote in 1870 that credit unions "are, according to paragraph eleven of the German law of cooperatives, "merchants" as defined by the common code of commerce. They accordingly form a sort of commercial business enterprise of which the owners are the [Credit] Unions' members".[31]

Corporate credit unions

Most credit unions provide service only to individual consumers. By contrast, *corporate credit unions* (also known as *central credit unions* in Canada) provide service to credit unions, with operational support, funds clearing tasks, and product and service delivery. The largest corporate credit union in the United States is U.S. Central Credit Union of Lenexa, Kansas, which serves as a central clearing house for other corporate credit unions and holds approximately $45.3 billion in assets.[32]

Leagues and associations

The World Council of Credit Unions is both a trade association for credit unions worldwide and a development agency. WOCCU's mission is to "assist its members and potential members to organize, expand, improve and integrate credit unions and related institutions as effective instruments for the economic and social development of all people".[33]

Credit unions in the United States have traditionally used a state/national trade association relationship that aligns credit unions with state "Credit Union Leagues" followed by national affiliation with the Credit Union National Association (CUNA) of Madison, Wisconsin. Federal credit unions may also be members of the National Association of Federal Credit Unions (NAFCU).

Credit unions with a specific focus on serving low- and moderate income people and communities, most of which are typically low-income designated by the National Credit Union Administration (NCUA), often join the New York, New York-based National Federation of Community Development Credit Unions (Federation), a national trade association providing investments, technical assistance, education and training and advocacy for community development credit unions (CDCUs) nationwide.

The Credit Union Executives Society (CUES), based in Madison, Wisconsin, provides professional development and resources to thousands of credit union executives and directors worldwide. It partners with world-renowned universities to offer graduate-level executive education specifically for credit union leaders.

The biggest UK credit union trade association is the Association of British Credit Unions Limited, more commonly known as Association of British Credit Unions, ABCUL. A significant number of credit unions are affiliated to ACE Credit Union Services (ACECUS) or UK Credit Unions (UKCU). Many Scottish credit unions are represented by the Scottish League of Credit Unions (SLCU) which has headquarters in Glasgow; however the majority of larger credit unions choose ABCUL.

Credit Union Central of Canada is the trade association for Canada's credit unions outside Quebec. The Desjardins Group represents Quebec's credit unions. Structurally, it blends the functions of a trade association and a more European-style cooperative bank.

Credit Unions often form cooperatives among themselves to provide services to members. A Credit Union Service Organization (CUSO) is generally a for-profit subsidiary of one or more credit unions formed for this purpose. For example, CO-OP Financial Services, the largest credit union owned interbank network in the US, provides an ATM network and shared branching services to credit unions. Other examples of cooperatives among credit unions include credit counseling services as well as insurance and investment services.

In New Zealand, most credit unions are affiliated to the New Zealand Association of Credit Unions.

United Kingdom

Credit unions in the United Kingdom have a long history. Identical or similar institutions to the present-day credit union were known as mutual societies within the United Kingdom.

Institutions known as mutual societies grew out of the friendly society movement of the 18th century, with the first mutual insurer, Equitable Life, being founded in 1762. The emergence of mutual assurance was linked with the Industrial Revolution and the need to provide for impoverished workers beyond the outmoded Elizabethan Poor Laws, as people congregated in the cities and lived in conditions of squalor and poverty. The principle of mutuality goes back to this epoch, when the sophisticated financial institutions taken for granted today, did not exist.

The only method of improving the quality of ordinary people's lives was through the development of co-operative and mutual societies, as formalised under the Friendly Societies Act 1819. Mutual institutions thus predated the welfare state and were formed to meet the needs of a burgeoning working class, consisting mainly of rural and immigrant workers. As a practical expression, this communitarian self-help movement allowed small regular individual contributions to be pooled for mutual collective benefit, obtaining the same economies of scope and scale necessary in providing collective insurance and banking products, to mitigate enduring social exclusion. Initially funding was required for housing, consumer durables and emergency insurance provision, at a time when commercial banks were still exclusively commercial lenders.[34]

Building societies were formed as small temporary societies by worker co-operatives, pooling resources to build local houses and subsequently allocating them among members by drawing lots. Once all members were housed, these organisations were typically wound up, although some became permanent societies in an effort to promote wider home ownership, as exemplified by the Leeds Permanent Building Society, see.[35] Surplus funds were then pooled, providing an opportunity for low-income families to earn interest on small deposits, with proceeds typically invested in residential mortgages and liquid government securities.

The traditional intermediation function of mutual societies was to promote thrift among the working classes and thereby provide access to low cost home loans. This ethos has become obscured in the recent battle for customers, and only the very real threat of extinction has occasioned any renewed vigour in proclaiming the original mutuality message. Mutual societies continue to perform vital social functions, often serving on the boards of local community groups, as well as regularly making sizeable local charitable donations. Indeed, the mutual legacy of social benefaction, although quite substantial, risks only being missed by the present generation once such institutions ultimately cease to exist.[36] With the conversion of most of the larger remaining mutual societies into proprietary companies, the bulk of the UK savings assets will have shifted away from their traditional providers into the mainstream UK financial sector. This change is occurring even as the traditional barriers between banks, building societies and insurance companies are disappearing. The spate of conversions is leading to a polarisation into two camps: the converters and the remaining mutuals.

Credit unions in the United Kingdom have been regulated by the Financial Services Authority since July 2002.[37] They are classified in two types: type 1 are the smaller credit unions while type 2 are larger. From November 2006 many type 2 credit unions began offering their members debit card accounts so that they could withdraw cash from any Link ATM.

In August 2010 the FSA will enact the CU-LRO (Credit Union - Legislative Reform Order) and widen access and modernise the powers of individual credit unions.

In October 2008 the Financial Services Compensation Scheme guaranteed the first 50,000 pounds of each saver's deposits in credit unions, in line with the guarantee for UK banks and building societies.[37] [38]

Credit unions in the UK now offer a wide range of services to their members; from direct debits to payroll deductions, from being able to send standing orders from their accounts to paying members bills to providing cheaper insurance facilities.[39] Life insurance is usually included with membership (subject to pre-existing medical conditions and other exclusions). Death benefits vary between unions, but commonly include lump sum payments, writing off of outstanding loans and doubling of savings.

Credit unions offer savers considerably more protection than commercial "savings clubs", as was demonstrated by the 2006 collapse of the Christmas hamper club Farepak.

In June 2008, the Treasury announced plans to encourage the growth of credit unions by broadening the common bond and removing outdated restriction. The changes are intended to significantly reduce the influence of door step lenders and loan sharks.[40]

Ireland

In June 2010, the Irish League of Credit Unions put forward plans to modernize the credit union system.[41]

Canada

Canada has the highest per-capita use of credit unions in North America, with more than a third of the population enrolled in one.[42] They are popular in Quebec, where they are known as *caisses populaires* (people's banks).[43]

Credit unions are called *caisses populaires* in French-speaking communities of Canada. This one is located in Shediac, New Brunswick

As of December 31, 2010, the Caisses Populaires Desjardins federated 451 member caisses with CAD$ 172.3 billion in assets and 5.8 million retail members, making it the sixth largest financial institution in Canada.[44]

Credit Union Central of Canada federates most credit unions in the English-speaking provinces. As of the end of 2009, the 10 affiliated systems operated 419 credit unions controlling CAD $122 billion in assets from 5.1 million retail members.[45] In British Columbia, 46 credit unions with assets of $48 billion, serve 1.7 million people.[45]

In Alberta, 46 independent credit unions, with 215 branches, serve more than 640,000 members. In Saskatchewan, 65 credit unions have 497,000 members and $12.2 billion in assets. Manitoba's 41 credit unions have 566,000 members with $17.5 billion in assets. In Ontario, 136 credit unions have 1.2 million members with $19.2 billion in assets.

Major Canadian credit unions include Vancity (Vancouver), Coast Capital Savings (Surrey), Envision Financial (Langley), Servus Credit Union (Edmonton), First Calgary Savings, Conexus Credit Union (Saskatchewan), Meridian Credit Union (Ontario), Libro Financial Group (London, Ontario) and Credit Union Atlantic (Halifax).

United States

In the United States, as of 2005 credit unions have 86 million members, which is 43.47% of the economically active population.[46] U.S. credit unions are not-for-profit, cooperative, tax-exempt organizations.[47] [48]

U.S. credit unions can be chartered by either the federal government ("federal credit unions")[49] or by a state.[50] The states of Delaware, South Dakota, and Wyoming do not regulate credit unions at the state level; in those states, a credit union must obtain a federal charter to operate.[51] All federal credit unions and 95% of state-chartered credit unions have "share insurance" (deposit insurance) of at least $250,000 per member through the National Credit Union Share Insurance Fund (NCUSIF).[52] [53] [54] This deposit insurance is backed by the full faith and credit of the United States government and is administered by the National Credit Union Administration.[53] As of December 2006, the NCUSIF had a higher insurance fund capital ratio than the fund for the Federal Deposit Insurance Corporation (FDIC).[55] U.S. credit unions also typically have higher equity capital ratios than U.S. banks.[55]

As of October 2011, the largest American credit union was Navy Federal Credit Union, serving U.S. Department of Defense employees, contractors, and families of servicepeople, with over $45 billion USD in assets and over 3.4 million members.[56]

Industry trade organizations include the American Credit Union Mortgage Association.

See also

- Bond of association
- Cooperative
- Democratic member control (cooperatives)
- Friedrich Wilhelm Raiffeisen
- History of credit unions
- World Council of Credit Unions
- Consumers' cooperative

References

[1] 12 U.S.C. § 1752(1), CUNA Model Credit Union Act § 0.20 (2007) (http://www.ncua.gov/RegulationsOpinionsLaws/fcu_act/fcu_act.pdf)

[2] 12 U.S.C. § 1757, CUNA Model Credit Union Act § 3.10 (2007) (http://www.ncua.gov/RegulationsOpinionsLaws/fcu_act/fcu_act.pdf)

[3] Sullivan, arthur; Steven M. Sheffrin (2003). *Economics: Principles in action* (http://www.pearsonschool.com/index.cfm?locator=PSZ3R9&PMDbSiteId=2781&PMDbSolutionId=6724&PMDbCategoryId=&PMDbProgramId=12881&level=4). Upper Saddle River, New Jersey 07458: Pearson Prentice Hall. p. 511. ISBN 0-13-063085-3. .

[4] "National Federation of Community Development Credit Unions, "What is a CDCU?"" (http://www.cdcu.coop/i4a/pages/index.cfm?pageid=261). Cdcu.coop. . Retrieved 2011-10-09.

[5] "Current Programs" (http://www.woccu.org/dev/programs/). WOCCU. . Retrieved 2011-10-09.

[6] "Publications" (http://www.woccu.org/dev/publications/). WOCCU. . Retrieved 2011-10-09.

[7] "Slide 1" (http://advice.cuna.org/download/combanks_cus.pdf) (PDF). . Retrieved 2011-10-09.

[8] "WOCCU, "What is a Credit Union?" (http://www.woccu.org/about/creditunion/). Woccu.org. . Retrieved 2011-10-09.

[9] for example the Ontario Credit Union Act, 1994 (as amended) c.11, s.24 (i)

[10] "CUNA, Products and Services, "Spanish Stuffer: Las Cooperativas de Ahorro y Crédito" (http://buy.cuna.org/detail.php?sku=21807). Buy.cuna.org. . Retrieved 2011-10-09.

[11] "DePeru, "Cooperativas de Ahorro y Crédito" (http://www.deperu.com/cooperativas/). Deperu.com. . Retrieved 2011-10-09.

[12] Caja Popular Mexicana, "Misión (you have to navigate to the "Misión" link) (http://www.cpm.org.mx/portal/CPMPortaldeInternet.nsf/CPMPILNFS001?OpenFrameSet)

[13] "Desjardins, "Liste de caisses par région" (http://www.desjardins.com/fr/votre_caisse/caisses-par-region.jsp) (in (**French**)). Desjardins.com. . Retrieved 2011-10-09.

[14] Banque Populaire de Rwanda, S.A., "Historique de l'UBPR (http://www.ubpr.co.rw/historique.htm)

[15] 12 U.S.C. § 1757(6), CUNA Model Credit Union Act § 0.70 (2007) (http://www.ncua.gov/RegulationsOpinionsLaws/fcu_act/fcu_act.pdf)

[16] 12 U.S.C. § 1760, CUNA Model Credit Union Act § 4.90 (2007) (http://www.ncua.gov/RegulationsOpinionsLaws/fcu_act/fcu_act.pdf)

[17] 12 U.S.C. §§ 1760-1761b, CUNA Model Credit Union Act §§ 5.15-5.20 (2007) (http://www.ncua.gov/RegulationsOpinionsLaws/fcu_act/fcu_act.pdf)

[18] "The Microfinance Gateway, "Credit Unions: Questions to Barry Lennon of WOCCU" (follow link to "Credit Unions: Questions to Barry Lennon of WOCCU")" (http://www.woccu.org/about/creditunion/). Woccu.org. . Retrieved 2011-10-09.

[19] World Council of Credit Unions, 2006 Statistical Report.

[20] European Association of Cooperative Banks, Annual Statistical Report, 2005.

[21] J. Carroll Moody & Gilbert C. Fite. *The Credit Union Movement: Origins and Development 1850 to 1980.* Kendall/Hunt Publishing Co., Dubuque, Iowa, 1984, p. 4

[22] J. Carroll Moody & Gilbert C. Fite. *The Credit Union Movement: Origins and Development 1850 to 1980.* p. 8

[23] "St. Mary's Credit Union" (http://www.abettercreditunion.com). . Retrieved 2009-08-24.

[24] Compare "not-for-profit", definition B, noun, Oxford English Dictionary (2008) ("An organization, corporation, etc., which does not operate for the purpose of making a profit".), with "non-profit", definition A(2), noun, Oxford English Dictionary (2008) ("A non-profit-making organization; spec. a charity".).

[25] "not-for-profit", definition A, adjective, Oxford English Dictionary (2008) ("Designating an organization, corporation, etc., which does not operate for the purpose of making a profit. Cf. NON-PROFIT, adj., FOR-PROFIT adj"

[26] "WOCCU, "What is a Credit Union?" ("As not-for-profit cooperative institutions, credit unions use excess earnings to offer members more affordable loans, a higher return on savings, lower fees or new products and services"" (http://www.woccu.org/about/creditunion/). Woccu.org. . Retrieved 2011-10-09.

[27] "The Microfinance Gateway, "Credit Unions: Questions to Barry Lennon of WOCCU" (follow link to "Credit Unions: Questions to Barry Lennon of WOCCU") ("Credit unions don't try to maximize profitability by charging high fees or rates of interest because they are owned by the people who use their services"" (http://www.woccu.org/about/creditunion). Woccu.org. . Retrieved 2011-10-09.

[28] "WOCCU, "PEARLS: Ratios: R - Rate of Return and Costs & S - Signs of Growth" (http://www.woccu.org/dev/pearls/pearlsratios). Woccu.org. . Retrieved 2011-10-09.
[29] The Microfinance Gateway, "Credit Unions: Questions to Barry Lennon of WOCCU" (http://www.woccu.org/about/creditunion/) (follow link to "Credit Unions: Questions to Barry Lennon of WOCCU")]
[30] "WOCCU, "PEARLS: Ratios: R - Rate of Return and Costs& S - Signs of Growth" (http://www.woccu.org/dev/pearls/pearlsratios/). Woccu.org. . Retrieved 2011-10-09.
[31] F.W. Raiffeisen. **The Credit Unions**. Trans. by Konrad Engelmann. The Raiffeisen Printing and Publishing Company, Neuwid on the Rhine, Germany, 1970.
[32] "U.S. Central FCU, "About U.S. Central" (http://www.uscentral.org/default.asp?content=about). Uscentral.org. . Retrieved 2011-10-09.
[33] "Mission" (http://www.woccu.org/about/mission/). WOCCU. . Retrieved 2009-11-25.
[34] Shay (1992)
[35] Anonymous (1994b)
[36] according to Stahl (1995)
[37] ABCUL (http://www.abcul.org/page/about/regulation.cfm). Retrieved 2008-10-17.
[38] FSCS FSCS - Consumer home page - Consumer Key Facts - Limitations of the scheme - Compensation Limits (http://www.fscs.org.uk/consumer/key_facts/limitations_of_the_scheme/compensation_limits/). Retrieved 2008-10-17.
[39] British Government to Place Stricter Controls on Credit Unions. (http://www.accessmylibrary.com/article-1G1-120512282/british-government-place-stricter.html) *Daily Mail.* 10 March 2002.
[40] Credit union rules 'to be eased'. (http://news.bbc.co.uk/2/hi/business/7480418.stm) *BBC News.* 30 June 2008.
[41] Stabilisation support to 'modernise' Credit Union (http://www.insideireland.ie/index.cfm/section/news/ext/creditunions001/category/1084)
[42] World Council of Credit Unions
[43] Desjardins: a model for the rest of Canada? (Quebec's Desjardins caisses populaires). (http://www.accessmylibrary.com/article-1G1-54036863/desjardins-model-rest-canada.html) *Canadian Banker.* 1 Jan. 1999.
[44] Desjardins Group. Desjardins Group figures (http://www.desjardins.com/en/a_propos/qui-nous-sommes/chiffres.jsp).
[45] Credit Union Central of Canada. (http://cucentral.ca/Default.aspx?DN=77211ee6-5d6b-4c58-a987-8f844c65c9cf).
[46] 2005 statistical report (http://www.woccu.org/_assets/documents/publications/2005StatisticalReport_English.pdf) from the World Council of Credit Unions
[47] CUNA Model Credit Union Act § 0.20 (2007) 26 U.S.C. § 501(c)(14)(A) for state-chartered credit unions and 26 U.S.C. § 501(c)(1) for federally-chartered credit unions (http://www.law.cornell.edu/uscode/html/uscode26/usc_sec_26_00000501----000-.html;)
[48] 12 U.S.C. §§ 1751 note, 1752(1), 1768 (http://www.ncua.gov/RegulationsOpinionsLaws/fcu_act/fcu_act.pdf)
[49] 12 U.S.C. §§ 1751-1772d (http://www.ncua.gov/RegulationsOpinionsLaws/fcu_act/fcu_act.pdf)
[50] Massachusetts General Laws chapter 171, §§ 1-84 (2008).
[51] Consumer Complaints and Hotline. (http://www.ncua.gov/resources/ConsumerInformation/Complaints/index.aspx) *National Credit Union Administration.*
[52] "NASCUS State-Chartered Credit Union Facts & Figures" (http://www.nascus.org/facts_figures_archive/12_31_07_FactsFigures.pdf) (PDF). National Association of State Credit Union Supervisors. 2007-12-31. . Retrieved 2008-07-19.
[53] NCUA, "Share Insurance (http://www.ncua.gov/ShareInsurance/index.htm)
[54] 12 U.S.C. §§ 1781-1790d (http://www.ncua.gov/RegulationsOpinionsLaws/fcu_act/fcu_act.pdf)
[55] "CUNA, "Frequently Requested U.S. Credit Union/Bank Comparisons" (http://advice.cuna.org/download/freq_compar.pdf) (PDF). . Retrieved 2011-10-09.
[56] "Navy Federal official web site" (https://www.navyfcu.org/about/about.php). . Retrieved 2010-10-21.

Further reading

- Ian MacPherson. *Hands Around the Globe: A History of the International Credit Union Movement and the Role and Development of the World Council of Credit Unions, Inc.* Horsdal & Schubart Publishers Ltd, 1999.
- F.W. Raiffeisen. *The Credit Unions.* Trans. by Konrad Engelmann. The Raiffeisen Printing and Publishing Company, Neuwid on the Rhine, Germany, 1970.
- Fountain, Wendell. *The Credit Union World.* AuthorHouse, Bloomington, Indiana, 2007. ISBN 978-1-4259-7006-2

External links

- Credit Union Database (http://www.creditunionsdb.com/) - all credit unions in USA
- World Council of Credit Unions (http://www.woccu.org/) trade association for credit unions
- Association of Asian Confederations of Credit Unions (http://www.aaccu.coop) regional federation representing 21 national federations in Asia with 35 million retail members
- Association of British Credit Unions Limited (http://www.abcul.org) - the largest trade body representing credit unions in the UK
- National Association of Credit Union Workers (http://www.nacuw.org.uk) - a staff association for all UK credit union workers regardless of trade body affiliation
- National Federation of Community Development Credit Unions (http://www/cdcu.coop/) - a trade body representing more than 240 community development credit unions (CDCUs) across the United States.
- Scottish League of Credit Unions (http://www.scottishcu.org/) - a trade body representing credit unions in Scotland
- ACE Credit Union Services (http://acecus.org/) - a trade body representing many smaller credit unions in the UK
- UK Credit Unions (http://www.ukcu.co.uk/) - a trade body representing many smaller credit unions in the UK

San Antonio

City of San Antonio

— City —

Flag

Seal

Nickname(s): River City, San Antone, Alamo City, Countdown City

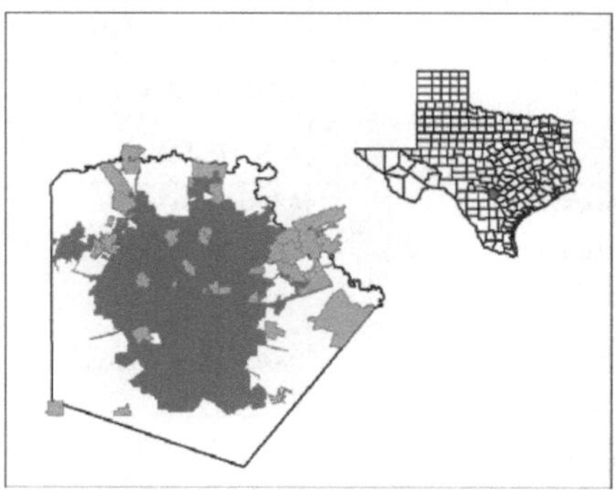

Location in the state of Texas

City of San Antonio

Location in the United States

Coordinates: 29°25′N 98°30′W	
Country	United States
State	Texas
County	Bexar, Medina
Government	
- Type	Council-Manager
- City Council	Mayor Julian Castro[1] Diego M. Bernal Ivy R. Taylor Jennifer V. Ramos Rey Saldaña David Medina, Jr. Ray Lopez Cris Medina W. Reed Williams Elisa Chan Carlton Soules
- City Manager	Sheryl Sculley
Area	
- City	412.1 sq mi (1067.3 km^2)
- Land	407.6 sq mi (1055.7 km^2)
- Water	4.5 sq mi (11.7 km^2)
Elevation	650 ft (198 m)
Population (2010)	
- City	1,327,408 (7th)
- Density	3400.9/sq mi (1313.1/km^2)
- Metro	2,142,508 (25th)
- Demonym	San Antonian
Time zone	Central (UTC-6)
- Summer (DST)	Central (UTC-5)
Area code(s)	210(majority), 830(portions)
Website	www.sanantonio.gov [2]

San Antonio (/ˌsænænˈtoʊni.oʊ/) is the seventh-largest city in the United States of America and the second-largest city within the state of Texas, with a population of 1.33 million.[3] Located in the American Southwest and the south–central part of Texas, the city serves as the seat of Bexar County. In 2011, it was estimated to be the 24th largest metropolitan area in the U.S. with a population of 2.2 million according to U.S. Census Bureau figures tabulated by Business First. San Antonio has characteristics of other western urban centers in which there are sparsely populated areas and a low density rate outside of the city. It was the fourth-fastest growing large city in the nation from 2000 to 2006[4] and the fifth-fastest-growing from 2007 to 2008.[5] The San Antonio–New Braunfels metropolitan area has a population of over 2.14 million based on the 2010 U.S. Census, making it the 25th-largest metropolitan area in the United States and third-largest in Texas.

The city was named for San Antonio de Padua, whose feast day is on June 13, when a Spanish expedition stopped in the area in 1691. Famous for Spanish missions, the Alamo, the River Walk, the Tower of the Americas, the Alamo Bowl, Marriage Island and host to SeaWorld and Six Flags Fiesta Texas theme parks, the city is visited by approximately 26 million tourists per year according to the San Antonio Convention and Visitors Bureau. The city is home to the four-time NBA champion San Antonio Spurs and the annual San Antonio Stock Show & Rodeo, one of the largest in the country.

San Antonio has a strong military presence—it is home to Fort Sam Houston, Lackland Air Force Base, Randolph Air Force Base, and Brooks City-Base, with Camp Bullis and Camp Stanley outside the city. Kelly Air Force Base operated out of San Antonio until 2001, when the airfield was transferred over to Lackland AFB and the remaining portions of the base became Port San Antonio, an industrial/business park. San Antonio is home to five Fortune 500 companies and the South Texas Medical Center, the only medical research and care provider in the South Texas region.

History

Lithograph of San Antonio in 1886.

Native Americans originally lived near the San Antonio River Valley, in the San Pedro Springs area, calling the vicinity "Yanaguana," meaning "refreshing waters." In 1691, a group of Spanish explorers and missionaries came upon the river and Native American settlement on June 13, the feast day of St. Anthony of Padua, Italy and named the place and river "San Antonio" in his honor.[6]

Early Spanish settlement of San Antonio began with the Martin de Alarcon expedition and the establishment of the San Antonio de Valero Mission (now the Alamo) as a means to reassert Spanish dominance over Texas from the nearby French in Louisiana. The viceroy, at the instigation of Father Antonio de San Buenaventura y Olivares, made the suppression of illicit trade from Louisiana a primary objective. He also pledged support for the Franciscan missions in Texas. Father Olivares had earlier visited a site on the San Antonio River in 1709, and from that time forward he was determined to found a mission and civilian settlement there. The viceroy gave formal approval for a halfway mission and presidio in late 1716, and assigned responsibility for their establishment to Martin de Alarcón, the governor of Coahuila and Texas. A series of delays, however, occasioned in part by differences between Alarcón and Olivares, postponed definitive action until 1718.[7] The families clustered around the presidio and mission formed the beginnings of Villa de Béxar, destined to become the most important town in Spanish Texas.[8] On May 1, on the San Antonio River, the governor founded Mission San Antonio de Valero (later famous as the Alamo), and on May 5 established Presidio San Antonio de Béxar. Presidio defending walls or breastworks would never be completed or necessary, as the mission itself would later become the principal unit of walled defense. San Antonio de Béxar Presidio, the center of Spanish defense in western Texas, was founded by Martín de Alarcón on May 5, 1718, on the west side of the San Antonio River one-fourth league from the San Antonio de Valero Mission.[7]

On February 14, 1719, the Marquis of San Miguel de Aguayo made a report to the king of Spain proposing that 400 families be transported from the Canary Islands, Galicia, or Havana to populate the province of Texas. His plan was approved, and notice was given the Canary Islanders (isleños) to furnish 200 families; the Council of the Indies suggested that 400 families should be sent from the Canaries to Texas by way of Havana and Veracruz. By June 1730, twenty-five families had reached Cuba and ten families had been sent on to Veracruz before orders from Spain to stop the movement arrived. Under the leadership of Juan Leal Goraz, the group marched overland to the presidio of San Antonio de Béjar (then spelled as "Bexar," a homonym city in Spain), where they arrived on March 9, 1731. The party had increased by marriages on the way to fifteen families, a total of fifty-six persons. They joined a military community that had been in existence since 1718. The immigrants formed the nucleus of the villa of **San Fernando de Béxar**, the first regularly organized civil government in Texas. Several of the old families of San Antonio trace their descent from the Canary Island colonists. María Rosa Padrón was the first baby born of Canary Islander descent in San Antonio.[9]

Memorial to the Alamo defenders

San Antonio grew to become the largest Spanish settlement in Texas, and for most of its history, the capital of the Spanish, later Mexican, province of Tejas. From San Antonio the Camino Real, today Nacogdoches Road in San Antonio, ran to the American border at the small frontier town of Nacogdoches. When Antonio López de Santa Anna unilaterally rescinded the Mexican Constitution of 1824 violence ensued in many states of Mexico. In a series of battles the Texian Army succeeded in forcing Mexican soldiers out of the settlement areas east of San Antonio. Under the leadership of Ben Milam, in the Battle of Bexar, December, 1835, Texian forces captured San Antonio from forces commanded by General Martin Perfecto de Cos, Santa Anna's brother in law. In the spring of 1836 Santa Anna marched on San Antonio. A volunteer force under the command of James C. Neill occupied and fortified the deserted mission. Upon his departure, the joint command of William Barrett Travis and James Bowie were left in charge of defending the old mission. The Battle of the Alamo took place from February 23 to March 6, 1836. The outnumbered Texian force was ultimately defeated, with all of the Alamo defenders killed. These men were seen as "martyrs" for the cause of Texas freedom and "Remember the Alamo" became a rallying cry in the Texian Army's eventual success at defeating Santa Anna's army.[10]

Juan Seguín, who organized the company of Hispanic patriots, that fought and died for Texas independence at the Battle of the Alamo, fought at the Battle of Concepcion, Siege of Bexar, and the Battle of San Jacinto, and served as mayor of San Antonio. He was forced out of that office, due to threats on his life, by sectarian newcomers and political opponents in 1842, becoming the last Hispanic mayor for nearly 150 years.[11]

Aerial view of the city, San Antonio, December 4, 1939

In 1845, the United States finally decided to annex Texas and include it as a state in the Union. This led to the Mexican-American War. Though the U.S. ultimately won, the war was devastating to San Antonio, and, at its end, the population of the city had been reduced by almost two thirds, to only 800 inhabitants.[12] By 1860, at the start of the Civil War, San Antonio had grown to a city of 15,000 people.

Following the Civil War, San Antonio prospered as a center of the cattle industry. During this period, San Antonio remained a frontier city, but its mixture of cultures also gave it a reputation as being beautiful and exotic. Frederick Law Olmstead, the architect who designed Central Park in New York City, once described San Antonio as having a, "jumble of races, costumes, languages, and buildings," which gave it a quality which only New Orleans could rival in, "odd and antiquated foreignness."[13]

In 1877, the first railroad reached San Antonio and the city was no longer on the frontier but began to enter the mainstream of American society. At the beginning of the 20th century, the streets of downtown were widened to accommodate street cars and modern traffic, destroying many historic buildings in the process.[14]

Like many municipalities in the American Southwest, San Antonio experiences steady population growth. The city's population has nearly doubled in 35 years, from just over 650,000 in the 1970 census to an estimated 1.2 million in 2005 through both steady population growth and land annexation (considerably enlarging the physical area of the city).

Geography

San Antonio is located near 29.5°N 98.5°W. According to the United States Census Bureau, in 2000 the city had a total area of 412.07 square miles (1067.3 km^2)—407.56 square miles (1055.6 km^2) (98.9%) of land and 4.51 square miles (11.7 km^2) (1.1%) of water. The city sits on the Balcones Escarpment.The altitude of San Antonio is 772 feet (235 m) above sea level.

The primary source of drinking water for the city is the Edwards Aquifer. Impounded in 1962 and 1969, respectively, Victor Braunig Lake and Calaveras Lake were among the first reservoirs in the country built to use recycled treated wastewater for power plant cooling, reducing the amount of groundwater needed for electrical generation.

Neighborhoods

Further information: Neighborhoods of San Antonio

Further information: Downtown San Antonio

Climate

San Antonio lies near the western edge of the humid subtropical climate zone. Its weather is alternately dry or humid depending on prevailing winds, turning hot in the summer, warm to cool winters subject to descending northern cold fronts in the winter with cool to cold nights, and comfortably warm and rainy in the spring and fall. San Antonio receives about a dozen sub-freezing nights each year, occasionally (about once every couple of winters) seeing some sort of wintry precipitation (i.e. sleet/freezing rain), but accumulation and snow itself is not very common. Many winters may pass without any freezing precipitation at all. According to the National Weather Service, there have been 31 instances of snowfall (a trace or more) in the city in the past 122 years, for an average of about once every four years. However a decade or more may pass between snowfalls.[15] In San Antonio, July and August tie for the average warmest months with an average high of 95 degrees Fahrenheit (35 °C). The highest temperature ever to be recorded was 111 °F (44 °C) on September 5, 2000.[15] The average coolest month is January. The lowest recorded temperature ever was 0 °F (−18 °C) on January 31, 1949.[15] May, June, and October have quite a bit of precipitation. For the last 135 years, the average annual precipitation has been 29.05 inches (738 mm), with a maximum of 52.28 inches (1328 mm) and a minimum of 10.11 inches (256.8 mm) in one year.[16]

Culture

Further information: Culture of San Antonio

Demographics

Historical populations		
Census	**Pop.**	**%±**
1850	3488	—
1860	8235	136.1%
1870	12256	48.8%
1880	20550	67.7%
1890	37673	83.3%
1900	53321	41.5%
1910	96614	81.2%
1920	161379	67.0%
1930	231542	43.5%
1940	253854	9.6%
1950	408442	60.9%
1960	587718	43.9%
1970	654153	11.3%
1980	785940	20.1%
1990	935933	19.1%
2000	1144646	22.3%
2010	1327407	16.0%
historical data sources:[20]		

At the 2010 Census, there were 1,327,407 people residing in San Antonio, an increase of 16.0% since 2000.

According to the 2010 Census, 26.6% of the population was non-Hispanic White, 6.3% non-Hispanic Black or African American, 0.2% non-Hispanic American Indian and Alaska Native, 2.3% non-Hispanic Asian, 0.1% non-Hispanic Native Hawaiian and Other Pacific Islander, 0.2% from some other race (non-Hispanic) and 1.2% from two or more races (non-Hispanic). 63.2% of San Antonio's population was of Hispanic, Latino, or Spanish origin (they may be of any race).

According to the 2000 U.S. Census, the *city* had a population of 1,144,646,[21] ranking it the ninth-most populated city in the country. Due to San Antonio's low density rate and lack of significant population surrounding the city limits, the *metropolitan area* ranked just 30th in the U.S. with a population of 1,592,383.[22]

Subsequent population counts, however, indicate continued growth in the area. The 2010 U.S. Census showed the city's population at 1,327,407,[23] making it the second-most populous city and the third-most populous metro area in Texas, as well as the seventh-most populous city in the U.S. The 2010 U.S. Census count for the eight-county San Antonio–New Braunfels metropolitan area placed its population at 2,142,508[24] making it the third-most populous metro area in Texas and the 25th-most populous metro area in the U.S. The metropolitan area is bordered to the northeast by Austin–Round Rock–San Marcos, and the two metropolitan areas together combine to form a region of about 3.9 million people.

There are 405,474 households, and 280,993 families residing in San Antonio. The population density is 2,808.5 people per square mile (1,084.4 km^2). There are 433,122 housing units at an average density of 1,062.7 per square mile (410.3 km^2).

The age of the city's population is spread out with 28.5% under the age of 18, 10.8% from 18 to 24, 30.8% from 25 to 44, 19.4% from 45 to 64, and 10.4% who are 65 years of age or older. The median age is 32 years. In San Antonio, 48% of the population are males, and 52% of the population are females. For every 100 females there are 93.5 males. For every 100 females age 18 and over, there are 89.7 males.

The median income for a household in the city is $36,214, and the median income for a family is $53,100. Males have a median income of $30,061 versus $24,444 for females. The per capita income for the city is $17,487. 17.3% of the population and 14.0% of families are below the poverty line. Out of the total population, 24.3% of those under the age of 18 and 13.5% of those 65 and older are living below the poverty line.

According to the 2006–2008 American Community Survey, the racial composition of San Antonio was as follows:

- White: 68.9% (Non-Hispanic Whites: 28.9%)
- Black or African American: 6.6%
- American Indian: 0.6%
- Asian: 2.0%
- Native Hawaiian and Other Pacific Islander: 0.1%
- Some other race: 19.4%
- Two or more races: 2.4%

- Hispanic or Latino (of any race): 61.2%

Source:[25]

Economy

South Texas Medical Center

San Antonio has a diversified economy with four primary focuses: financial services, government, health care, and tourism. Located northwest of the city center is the South Texas Medical Center, which is a conglomerate of various hospitals, clinics, and research (see Southwest Research Institute) and higher educational institutions.

Headquarters of Valero Energy Corporation

The city is also home to one of the largest military concentrations in the United States. The defense industry in San Antonio employs over 89,000 and provides a $5.25 billion impact to the city's economy.[26]

Twenty million tourists visit the city and its attractions every year, contributing substantially to the city's economy.[27] The Henry B. Gonzalez Convention Center alone hosts more than 300 events each year with over 750,000 convention delegates from around the world. Tourism employs 94,000 citizens and makes an economic impact of over $10.7 billion in the local economy as revealed in the Economic Impact Study conducted every two years by the San Antonio Tourism Council and the research team of Dr. Richard Butler and Dr. Mary Stefl of Trinity University. Tourism also brings new annual revenues to the City of San Antonio and other governmental entities with the hotel & motel tax, sales taxes and other revenues from hospitality agreements and contracts. This number exceeded over $160 million in the 2004 study.

Of the 140 Fortune Global 500 companies headquartered in the US, San Antonio is home to two: Valero Energy Corp #33, and Tesoro Petroleum Corp #317.

San Antonio is home to five Fortune 500 companies: Valero Energy Corp, Tesoro, USAA, Clear Channel Communications and NuStar Energy.[28] H-E-B, the 19th largest private company in the United States[29] is also headquartered in San Antonio. Other companies headquartered in San Antonio are: Kinetic Concepts, Frost National Bank, Harte-Hanks, Eye Care Centers of America, Bill Miller Bar-B-Q Enterprises, Taco Cabana, Whataburger, and Rackspace.

Other large companies that operate regional headquarters in the city include: Nationwide Mutual Insurance Company, Kohl's, Allstate, Chase Bank, Philips, Wells Fargo, Toyota, Medtronic, Sysco, Caterpillar Inc., AT&T, West Corporation, Citigroup, Boeing, QVC, and Lockheed Martin.

In between the beginning of 1997 and March 11, 1998, San Antonio lost several major company headquarters. In 1997 Titan Holdings and USLD Communications had sold their operations to larger companies. After a Los Angeles buyout specialist purchased Builders Square, the company's operations were moved out of San Antonio.[30]

Attractions

San Antonio is a popular tourist destination. The jewel of the city is the River Walk, which meanders through the downtown area. Lined with numerous shops, bars, and restaurants, as well as the Arneson River Theater, this attraction is transformed into an impressive festival of lights during the Christmas and New Year holiday period, and is suffused with the local sounds of folklorico and flamenco music during the summer, particularly during celebrations such as the Fiesta Noche del Rio. Also based along the River Walk is the newly restored Aztec On The River, the only surviving exotic-themed movie palace in Texas.

The Alamo, located nearby, is Texas' top tourist attraction, while the River Walk is the second most visited attraction. SeaWorld, located 16 miles (26 km) west of downtown, is the number 3 attraction. Also, there is the very popular Six Flags Fiesta Texas. Morgan's Wonderland is a theme park for special needs children.

The downtown area also features Cathedral of San Fernando, The Majestic Theatre, HemisFair Park (home of the Tower of the Americas and the Institute of Texan Cultures), La Villita, El Mercado, the Spanish Governor's Palace, and the historic Menger Hotel. On the northern side of the Alamo complex, beside the Emily Morgan Hotel, is the San Antonio Cavalry Museum, which features cavalry artifacts and exhibits and is frequented by local re-enactors.

The Fairmount Hotel, built in 1906 and San Antonio's second oldest hotel, is in the *Guinness World Records* as one of the heaviest buildings ever moved intact. It was placed in its new location, three blocks south of the Alamo, over four days in 1985, and cost $650,000 to move.

The Alamo, San Antonio's most famous attraction

The River Walk around Christmastime

The *Torch of Friendship* sculpture

San Antonio's historic River Walk extends some 2½ miles, attracting several million visitors every year.

Another view of the city's downtown area

Central Library of The San Antonio Public Library

The Tower of the Americas characterizes the city's skyline

The historic Bexar County Courthouse

The San Antonio Convention Center

The Shops at La Cantera is a non-enclosed shopping mall located near the University of Texas at San Antonio in the northwestern portion of the city.

The San Antonio Botanical Garden

San Antonio Missions National Historical Park

SeaWorld San Antonio

Aztec On The River Theater

Six Flags Fiesta Texas

IMAX Theater

Henry B. Gonzalez Convention Center

San Antonio is home to the first museum of modern art in Texas, the McNay Art Museum. Other places of interest include The Woodlawn Theatre, the San Antonio Zoo, the Japanese Tea Gardens, Kumamoto, Brackenridge Park, the missions of the San Antonio Missions National Historical Park, the Museo Alameda, the San Antonio Museum of Art, the Witte Museum, the Texas Rangers Museum, the Buckhorm Museum, ArtPace, Blue Star Contemporary Art Center, SeaWorld San Antonio, Six Flags Fiesta Texas, the Texas Transportation Museum, and Splashtown San Antonio. Visitors can also experience something of the cowboy culture year round, they can see the 40-foot (12 m) tall cowboy boots at North Star Mall.

Beyond taking in the sights and sounds of San Antonio, tourists can sample some of its world famous Tex-Mex cuisine at the many fine restaurants located throughout the city. Mexican restaurants are abundant in virtually all parts of town, and most are relatively inexpensive. Some outstanding examples of Tex-Mex eateries include Jacala, on West Avenue on the near Northwest side, La Hacienda de Los Barrios, on the North East side, Tommy's on Nogalitos at I-35 near downtown, and Los Barrios, on the near North side of town.

Sports

Sport	League	Club	Founded	Venue	League championships	Championship years
Basketball	NBA	San Antonio Spurs	1967	AT&T Center	4	1999, 2002–03, 2004–05, 2006–07
Basketball	WNBA	San Antonio Silver Stars	1997	AT&T Center	0	N/A
Hockey	AHL	San Antonio Rampage	2002	AT&T Center	0	N/A
Baseball	TL	San Antonio Missions	1968	Nelson W. Wolff Municipal Stadium	12	1897, 1903, 1908, 1933, 1950, 1961, 1964, 1997, 2002, 2003, 2007, 2011
Soccer	NASL	San Antonio Scorpions	2010	Heroes Stadium	0	N/A
Arena Football	AFL	San Antonio Talons	2000	Alamodome	2	2003, 2007

The city's only top-level professional sports team, and consequently the team most San Antonians follow, is the San Antonio Spurs of the National Basketball Association. Previously, the Spurs played at the Alamodome, which was built for football, and before that the HemisFair Arena, but the Spurs built—with public money—and moved into the SBC Center in 2002, since renamed the AT&T Center.

The AT&T Center

The AT&T Center is also home to the San Antonio Rampage of the American Hockey League and the San Antonio Silver Stars of the WNBA, both owned by the Spurs Organization. San Antonio is home to the Double-A Minor League affiliate of the San Diego Padres, the San Antonio Missions who play at Nelson Wolff Stadium on the west side of the city. (San Antonio is the largest city in the country with neither a Major League nor AAA baseball team.) San Antonio hosts the NCAA football Alamo Bowl each December.

San Antonio has two rugby union teams, the Alamo City Rugby Football Club, and San Antonio Rugby Football Club.

The city is also home to St. Mary's University and the University of Texas San Antonio who field the only two collegiate Mens Rugby teams in the city. Both schools compete in Division III Texas Rugby Union, both schools are city and division rivals.

The University of Texas at San Antonio fields San Antonio's only NCAA Division I athletic teams known as the UTSA Roadrunners. The University recently added football, hiring former University of Miami coach Larry Coker as its initial head coach. Roadrunner football will begin play in 2011.

The city is also home of the U.S. Army All-American Bowl,[31] played annually in the Alamodome and televised live on NBC. The Bowl is an East versus West showdown featuring the nation's top 90 high school senior football players. The game has featured NFL stars Reggie Bush, Vince Young, Adrian Peterson, and many other college and NFL stars.

City officials are said to be attempting to lure the National Football League permanently to San Antonio and have also said that a strong showing at the Alamodome for the three local Saints games was vital to showing that San Antonio can support an NFL franchise. NFL Commissioner Paul Tagliabue stated San Antonio was successful in hosting the team, and that the city would be on the short list for any future NFL expansions. The city has also hosted the Dallas Cowboys and Houston Oilers preseason camps in the past, and they have signed a contract with the Cowboys in which the Cowboys will practice in San Antonio through 2011.[32] Cowboys owner Jerry Jones has acknowledged his support for the city's efforts to become home to an NFL franchise.[33] Although it is the second largest city in the United States without an NFL team (after Los Angeles), San Antonio's smaller metropolitan population has so far contributed to its lack of landing an NFL, MLB, or NHL team.

The city got its first professional soccer team, the San Antonio Scorpions of the North American Soccer League, in 2010. They are expected to begin playing in 2012 initially in Heroes Stadium pending the completion of a soccer-specific facility in the STAR Soccer Complex.

San Antonio will be getting a National Premier Soccer League expansion team in 2010.[34]

Government

Further information: List of mayors of San Antonio

The City of San Antonio runs under a Council-Manager form of government. The city is divided into 10 council districts designed to ensure equal population distribution between all districts. Each district elects one person to sit on the City Council with the mayor elected on a city-wide basis. All members of the City Council, which includes the mayor, are elected to two-year terms and are limited to four terms in total (except for those who were in office in November, 2008 and are limited to a total of two terms). Houston and Laredo have similar term limits to those in San Antonio. All positions are elected on non-partisan ballots as required by Texas law. Council members are paid $20 per meeting, while the Mayor earns $4,000 a year. Most council members maintain full-time employment in addition to their positions on the council.[35] The current mayor is Julian Castro.

The council hires the City Manager to handle day to day operations. The council effectively functions as the city's legislative body with the City Manager acting as its Chief Executive, responsible for the management of day to day operations and execution of council legislation. The current City Manager is Sheryl Sculley.

The city operates its own electric and gas utility service, CPS Energy.

The city stretches into several national congressional districts and is represented in Congress by the following:[36]

- Senate
  - Kay Bailey Hutchison (R)
  - John Cornyn (R)
- House of Representatives
  - Texas District 20: Charlie Gonzalez (D)
  - Texas District 21: Lamar Smith (R)
  - Texas District 23: Quico Canseco (R)
  - Texas District 28: Henry Cuellar (D)
- State Governor
  - Rick Perry (R)

Growth policy

Unlike most large cities in the U.S., San Antonio is not completely surrounded by independent suburban cities, and under Texas law[37] it exercises extraterritorial jurisdiction (ETJ) over much of the surrounding unincorporated land,[38] including planning major thoroughfares and enforcing rules for platting and subdivision. It pursues an aggressive annexation policy and opposes the creation of other municipalities within its ETJ.[39] Nearly three-fourths of its current land area has been annexed since 1960.[40] In the 2000s the city has annexed several long narrow corridors along major thoroughfares in outlying areas to facilitate eventual annexation of growth developing along the routes. The city planned to annex nearly forty additional square miles by 2009.[41] In May 2010, the San Antonio agreed to release thousands of acres of land in its extraterritorial jurisdiction along Interstate 10 to Schertz. The agreement releases a total of 3486 acres (14.11 km^2) of San Antonio's ETJ lands north of I-10 to Schertz. The ETJ lands are in an area bordered by FM 1518 to the west, Lower Seguin Road to the north, Cibolo Creek to the east and I-10 to the south. [42]

Involuntary annexation is a controversial issue in those parts of unincorporated Bexar County affected by it. Residents, attracted to the outlying areas by lower taxes and affordable real estate values, often see annexation as a mechanism to increase property tax rates (primarily driven by school district taxes) without a corresponding improvement in services such as police and fire protection, while the city regards its annexation policy as essential to its overall prosperity.[43]

State and federal representation

The Texas Department of Criminal Justice (TDCJ) operates the Parole Division Region IV headquarters in the San Antonio Metro Parole Complex. San Antonio district parole offices I and III are in the parole complex, while office II is in another location.[44]

The Texas Department of Transportation operates the San Antonio District Office in San Antonio.[45]

The United States Postal Service operates the San Antonio Main Post Office.[46] Other post offices are located throughout San Antonio.

Education

San Antonio hosts over 100,000 students across its 31 higher-education facilities which include The University of Texas Health Science Center at San Antonio, the University of Texas at San Antonio, Texas A&M University–San Antonio, and the Alamo Community College District. Some of the private schools include Baptist University of the Américas, St. Mary's University, Our Lady of the Lake University, University of the Incarnate Word, Trinity University, and Wayland Baptist University. The San Antonio Public Library serves all of these institutions along with the 17 school districts within San Antonio.

University of Texas at San Antonio

The city is also home to more than 30 private schools and charter schools. These schools include: Central Catholic Marianist High School, Incarnate Word High School, Saint Mary's Hall, The Atonement Academy, Antonian College Preparatory High School, San Antonio Academy, Holy Cross High School, Providence High School, The Carver Academy, Keystone School, TMI — The Episcopal School of Texas, St. Anthony Catholic High School, Lutheran High School of San Antonio, and Harmony Science Academy.

San Antonio is also home to U.S. Air Force Basic Military Training,. The Air Force only has one location for enlisted basic training: the 737th Training Group, at Lackland Air Force Base. All new Air Force recruits go through the same basic training at Lackland. Each year, over 35,000 new recruits go through AFBMT. METC, (Military Education and Training Campus) which is the U.S. Military Medical Training at Fort Sam Houston hosts 30 programs and over 24,000 annual graduates. It is the largest Medical education center in the world.

Transportation

Air

The San Antonio International Airport (**SAT**) is located in north central San Antonio, approximately eight miles from downtown. It has two terminals and is served by 21 airlines serving 43 destinations including three in Mexico. Stinson Municipal Airport is a reliever airport located six miles (10 km) south of downtown San Antonio's central business district. The airport has two runways and it is also home to the Texas Air Museum.

A VIA bus stopped at a downtown intersection

Mass transit

A bus and rubber tired streetcar (bus) system is provided by the city's metropolitan transit authority, VIA Metropolitan Transit. VIA's full fare monthly unlimited Big Pass is only $30 per month making VIA the most economically priced large transit authority in the nation. In August 2010, VIA Metropolitan Transit unveiled the next set of buses that are powered by diesel-electric hybrid technology. The 30 hybrid buses are being put into service on VIA's express routes to serve daily commuters across the city. This set of buses follows the introduction of new vehicles powered by compressed natural gas, which were unveiled in May 2010. In the fall of 2010, VIA will begin taking delivery of three new buses that will be powered by electricity from on-board batteries. These buses will service the downtown core area, and they will be the first revenue vehicles VIA operates that have zero emissions.[47] VIA offers 84 regular bus routes and three downtown streetcar routes. This includes express service from downtown to park and ride locations in the South, West, Northwest, North Central and Northeast areas of the city with service to UTSA, Six Flags Fiesta Texas and SeaWorld. VIA also offers a special service to city events including Spurs games and city parades from its park and ride locations. VIA has among its many routes, one of the longest local transit routes in the nation. Routes 550 (Clockwise) and 551 (Counterclockwise) travels 48 miles (77 km) one way as it loops around the city.[48] San Antonio became the largest city in the U.S. to not have a intra-city rail system when Phoenix, the former city that had this title, got such a system in 2008. VIA is currently in the process of creating a Bus Rapid Transit line known as VIA Primo.[49] A proposed passenger rail line, LSTAR, would link the city to Austin.[50]

Rail

Amtrak, the national passenger rail service, provides service to San Antonio at San Antonio Amtrak Station, operating its *Texas Eagle* daily between San Antonio and Chicago's Union Station.[51] Amtrak also operates its *Sunset Limited* three times a week in each direction through San Antonio between Los Angeles and Orlando, Florida (currently truncated to New Orleans due to the effects of Hurricane Katrina).[52] The *Texas Eagle* section travels between San Antonio and Los Angeles as part of the *Sunset Limited*. The old Sunset Station is now an entertainment venue owned by VIA and neighbored by the current station and the Alamodome.[53]

Road

San Antonio is served by these major freeways:

- Interstate 10: McDermott Freeway (Northwest) runs west toward El Paso, Phoenix and Los Angeles. Jose Lopez Freeway (East) runs east toward Seguin, Houston, New Orleans and Jacksonville
- Interstate 35: Pan Am Expressway (Northeast/Southwest)—runs south toward Laredo and runs north toward Austin, Dallas–Fort Worth, Oklahoma City, Kansas City and Minneapolis
- Interstate 37: Lucian Adams Freeway (Southeast)—runs from San Antonio through its junction with U.S. Highway 281 south (Edinburg and McAllen) near Three Rivers and into Corpus Christi through its junction with U.S. Highway 77 south (Kingsville, Harlingen and Brownsville) to its southern terminus at Corpus Christi Bay.
- Interstate 410: Connally Loop—simply called Loop 410 (four-ten) by locals is a 53-mile (85 km) inner beltway around the city.
- U.S. 90: Cleto Rodriguez Freeway (West) through Uvalde and Del Rio to its western terminus at I-10 in Van Horn. Prior to I-10 East and US 90 West expressway being built US 90 traveled through the west side via West Commerce St. (westbound) and Buena Vista St. (eastbound) and Old Hwy 90. On the east side it traveled along East Commerce St. to its current alignment which runs concurrent with I-10 East to Seguin.
- U.S. 281: McAllister Freeway (North) to Johnson City and Wichita Falls. Southbound, it runs concurrent with I-37, then I-410 for 4 miles (6 km), then heads south to Pleasanton. Prior to I-37 and McAllister Fwy. being built US 281 traveled through the north side via San Pedro Ave. and the south side via Roosevelt Ave.
- State Highway 151: Stotzer Freeway runs from US Hwy 90 West through Westover Hills which includes SeaWorld to its western terminus at State Loop 1604.

- State Loop 1604: Charles W. Anderson Loop—simply called 1604 (sixteen-oh-four) by locals—is a 96-mile (154 km) outer beltway around San Antonio

Other highways include:

- U.S. 87: Southbound to Victoria along Roland Avenue then Rigsby Avenue. It runs concurrent with I-10 for 52 miles (84 km) where it goes to San Angelo northbound.
- U.S. 181: Starts 0.5 miles (0.8 km) south of I-410/I-37/US 281 interchange and heads toward Corpus Christi via Beeville. Prior to I-37 being built US 181 traveled along Presa St. from downtown to its current alignment.
- State Highway 16: From Freer, it runs concurrent with I-410 for 17 miles (27 km) along southwest San Antonio, over to Bandera Road to Bandera.
- State Loop 345: Fredericksburg Road is the business loop for I-10 West/US-87 North.[54]
- State Loop 368: Broadway and Austin Highway is the business loop for I-35 North.[55]
- State Loop 353: Nogalitos Street and New Laredo Highway is the business loop for I-35 South.[56]
- State Loop 13: Is the city's inner loop on the south side serving Lackland AFB, Port San Antonio, South Park Mall and Brooks CityBase traveling along Military Dr. on the south side and WW White Rd. on the east side to its junction with I-35/I-410. The northern arc of the loop is now I-410.

Bicycle paths

San Antonio has approximately 136 miles (219 km) of bike lanes, routes or off-road paths.[57] Off-road trails travel along the San Antonio River, linear greenways, or city parks. Although largely disconnected, the progress to create a bicycle-friendly environment was recognized when San Antonio was designated a Bronze-Level Bicycle Friendly Community by the League of American Bicyclists.[58]

Bicycle sharing

A bike sharing service was approved by the city council on June 17, 2010.[59] The initial program will consist of 140 bikes at 14 locations supported by a "central hub" and is expected to serve both residents and visitors. San Antonio Bike Share, a non-profit, is being formed to oversee the operation, which will be locally operated and maintained by Bike World. B-Cycle, the same system being used in Denver, will be supplying the bike share system. It started operation March 2011.[60]

Walkability

A 2011 study by Walk Score ranked San Antonio the fortieth most walkable of fifty largest cities in the United States.[61]

Notable natives and residents

Further information: Notables of San Antonio, Texas

Media and entertainment

Print

San Antonio has one major newspaper, the *San Antonio Express-News*, which has served the area since 1865. Robert Rivard, who currently serves as the paper's executive vice president and editor,[62] was named Managing Editor in 1994 and then Editor in 1997. The *Express-News* currently circulates as the largest newspaper service in South Texas. The Hearst Corporation, which owned a second newspaper, the *San Antonio Light*, purchased the *Express-News* from News Corp. in 1992 and shut down the *Light* after failing to find a buyer. Hearst, using the Express-News brand, also produces *Conexion*, a weekly magazine written by an entirely Hispanic staff with a

Hispanic spin on weekly events. The San Antonio *Current* is the free "alternative" paper published weekly with local political issues, art and music news, restaurant listings and reviews, and listings of events and nightlife around town. In addition, the *San Antonio Business Journal* covers general business news. *La Prensa*, a bilingual publication, also has a long history in San Antonio. The *San Antonio River Walk Current* covers general San Antonio news.

Radio

See also: Broadcast media in San Antonio

FM: 28 **AM:** 20

About 50 radio stations can be heard in the San Antonio area — 30 of them are actually located in the city. San Antonio is home to Clear Channel Communications, the largest operator of radio stations in the U.S. Its flagship, WOAI AM-1200, is known for its local news operation, considered among the best in the country. The first radio station to broadcast in South Texas was KTSA AM-550 in 1922. Some of KTSA AM-550's better known local talk show hosts include Jack Riccardi, Trey Ware and Ricci Ware.

There are three National Public Radio stations in San Antonio, which belong to Texas Public Radio (www.TPR.org); KSTX 89.1 FM is NPR news/talk, KPAC 88.3 is a 24-hour classical music station, and KTXI 90.1 is a mix of NPR news/talk and classical music broadcast for the West Central Texas Hill County. KSTX also broadcasts "Riverwalk Jazz", featuring Jim Cullum Jazz Band at The Landing, a fixture on the River Walk since 1963. KRTU 91.7 is a non-commercial radio station based out of Trinity University. Unlike other college radio stations throughout the U.S. the station plays jazz 17 hours a day and college rock/indie rock at night. College Alternative station KSYM, 90.1 FM, is owned by the Alamo Community College District and operated by San Antonio College students and like KRTU it plays the Third Coast music network during the day and alternative music at night.

Most Latin stations in the area play regional Mexican, Tejano or contemporary pop. On January 12, 2006, Univision-owned KCOR-FM "La Kalle 95.1" changed its format from Hispanic-Rhythmic Contemporary Hits to Spanish Oldies, then named "Recuerdo 95.1". However, Univision announced on November 10, 2006, that it flipped KLTO Tejano 97.7's format to Reggaeton in an attempt to reintroduce the format to San Antonio again. Then, 97.7 was flipped again to feature a rock format. The station no longer broadcasts anything in English and while still owned by Univision, it now broadcasts music from artists such as Linkin Park. On the other hand, 95.1 was then flipped back to the "La Kalle" format again after being flipped more than a year ago to feature a "95X" format. KLTO was acquired earlier in the year and operated as a simulcast of KXTN Tejano 107.5. San Antonio has quickly diversified in recent years, with the influx of non-Tejano Latinos, mostly from the East Coast, who are serving in the city's various military bases, as well as immigrants from Mexico. Therefore, just like in the rest of the country, radio station conglomerates have been changing formats in San Antonio to reflect shifting demographics.

Television

While the city is one of the ten largest in the United States, its television market is only the 37th in the United States, according to marketing research firm ACNielsen.[63] This is primarily due to the relatively low population-density of the outlying areas and the close proximity of Austin, which truncates the potential market area. San Antonio-based TV stations are WOAI channel 4 (NBC), KSAT channel 12 (ABC), KENS channel 5 (CBS), KABB channel 29 (Fox Broadcasting Company), KCWX channel 2 (myNetworkTV), KMYS channel 35 (The CW) and KLRN channel 9 (PBS). The market is also home to six Spanish language stations, three religious stations, three

WOAI-TV is San Antonio's NBC affiliate

independent stations and one Internet-based station (210 TV [64]). The San Antonio market has 65% cable TV penetration.

Sister cities

- - Monterrey, Mexico (1953)[65]
- - Guadalajara, Mexico (1974)[65]
- - Las Palmas de Gran Canaria, Spain (1975)[65]
- - Kwangju, South Korea (1981)[65]
- - Kaohsiung, Taiwan (1981)[65]
- - Santa Cruz de Tenerife, Spain (1983)[65]
- - Kumamoto, Japan (1987)[65]
- - Chennai, India (2008)[66] [65]

Alliance/Friendship cities

- - Wuxi, Jiangsu, China (2010 friendship city)[65] [67]
- - Suzhou, Jiangsu, China) (2010 friendship city)[65] [68]
- - Dresden, Saxony, Germany (2009 alliance agreement)[65]
- - Tel Aviv, Israel (2011 economic pact)[69]

See also

- Chisholm Trail
- Fiesta San Antonio
- National Register of Historic Places listings in Bexar County, Texas

References

[1] "GOVERNMENT Links on the San Antonio Community Portal" (http://www.sanantonio.gov/mayor/indexcastro.asp). Sanantonio.gov. . Retrieved 2010-06-30.
[2] http://www.sanantonio.gov/
[3] Mildenberg, David (February 18, 2011). "Population growth in Texas eclipses national rate" (http://www.washingtonpost.com/wp-dyn/content/article/2011/02/17/AR2011021707179.html?nav=hcmoduletmv). *The Washington Post*. .
[4] Christie, Les (June 28, 2007). "The fastest growing U.S. cities - June 28, 2007" (http://money.cnn.com/2007/06/27/real_estate/fastest_growing_cities/). *CNN*. . Retrieved May 23, 2010.
[5] Ayala, Elaine (July 1, 2009). "S. A. Again Census Standout" (http://www.mysanantonio.com/news/local_news/SA_again_census_standout.html). *San Antonio Express News*. pp. B1. . Retrieved 2009-07-01.
[6] "San Antonio: The City of St. Anthony - June 2004 Issue of St. Anthony Messenger Magazine Online" (http://www.americancatholic.org/Messenger/Jun2004/Feature2.asp#F1). Americancatholic.org. . Retrieved 2010-06-30.
[7] (http://www.tshaonline.org/handbook/online/articles/SS/uqs8.html) Spanish Texas, Texas State Historical Society: The Handbook of Texas Online
[8] (http://www.tshaonline.org/handbook/online/articles/AA/fal2.html) Martin de Alarcon, Texas State Historical Society: The Handbook of Texas Online
[9] (http://www.tshaonline.org/handbook/online/articles/CC/poc1.html) The Canary Islanders, Texas State Historical Society: The Handbook of Texas Online
[10] John H. Jenkins, ed., Papers of the Texas Revolution (10 vols.; Austin: Presidial Press, 973),13
[11] Gonzalez, Juan. *Harvest of Empire*. Penguin, 2000.
[12] Fisher, Lewis F. (1996). *Saving San Antonio: the precarious preservation of a heritage*. Lubbock: Texas Tech University Press.
[13] A Journey Through Texas by Frederick Olmstead ISBN 978-1-144-80380-1
[14] Saving San Antonio by Lewis F. Fisher ISBN 978-0-89672-372-6
[15] "San Antonio Climate Summary" (http://www.srh.noaa.gov/images/ewx/sat/satclisum.pdf) (PDF). National Weather Service. . Retrieved August 19, 2010.

[16] "MONTHLY/ANNUAL/AVERAGE PRECIPITATION SAN ANTONIO, TX (1871–2010)" (http://www.srh.noaa.gov/images/ewx/sat/satmonrain.pdf) (PDF). National Weather Service. . Retrieved August 19, 2010.
[17] "NCDC: U.S. Climate Normals" (http://cdo.ncdc.noaa.gov/climatenormals/clim20/tx/417945.pdf). National Oceanic and Atmospheric Administration. . Retrieved 2010-04-20.
[18] "Average Weather for San Antonio, TX - Temperature and Precipitation" (http://www.weather.com/weather/wxclimatology/monthly/graph/USTX1200). The Weather Channel. . Retrieved 2010-04-20.
[19] "Climatological Normals of San Antonio" (http://www.hko.gov.hk/wxinfo/climat/world/eng/n_america/us/san_antonio_e.htm). Hong Kong Observatory. . Retrieved 2010-05-12.
[20] "1990 Population and Housing Unit Counts: United States (CPH-2)" (http://www.census.gov/prod/cen1990/cph2/cph-2-1-1.pdf). . Retrieved 2008-08-11.
[21] Census 2000: Incorporated Places of 100,000 or More, Ranked by Population (http://www.census.gov/population/cen2000/phc-t5/tab02.txt), U.S. Census Bureau.
[22] Census 2000: Metropolitan Areas Ranked by Population (http://www.census.gov/population/cen2000/phc-t3/tab03.txt), U.S. Census Bureau.
[23] (http://www.census.gov/popest/cities/tables/SUB-EST2008-01.csv), U.S. Census Bureau.
[24] (http://www.census.gov/Press-Release/www/releases/archives/cb07-51tbl1.pdf), U.S. Census Bureau.
[25] American FactFinder, United States Census Bureau. "San Antonio city, Texas - ACS Demographic and Housing Estimates: 2006–2008" (http://factfinder.census.gov/servlet/ADPTable?_bm=y&-geo_id=16000US4865000&-qr_name=ACS_2008_3YR_G00_DP3YR5&-ds_name=ACS_2008_3YR_G00_&-_lang=en&-_sse=on). Factfinder.census.gov. . Retrieved 2010-06-30.
[26] "Welcome to the City of San Antonio Economic Development Department-Index" (http://www.sanantonio.gov/edd/). Sanantonio.gov. . Retrieved 2010-06-30.
[27] San Antonio Tourism (http://www.sanantonioriverwalk.com/tourism.html), San Antonio Riverwalk.com. Retrieved January 7, 2007.
[28] "Fortune 500 2009: States: Texas Companies" (http://money.cnn.com/magazines/fortune/fortune500/2009/states/TX.html). *CNN*. . Retrieved May 23, 2010.
[29] "America's Largest Private Companies" (http://www.forbes.com/lists/2009/21/private-companies-09_Americas-Largest-Private-Companies_Rank.html). Forbes.com. October 28, 2009. . Retrieved 2010-06-30.
[30] Nowlin, Sanford. " Aquila bids for sale or merger (http://nl.newsbank.com/nl-search/we/Archives?p_product=SAEC&p_theme=saec&p_action=search&p_maxdocs=200&p_topdoc=1&p_text_direct-0=0EAFE82B06042C69&p_field_direct-0=document_id&p_perpage=10&p_sort=YMD_date:D&s_trackval=GooglePM)." *San Antonio Express-News*. March 11, 1998. Business 1E. Published in: Polishuk, Paul. *Utilities Telecommunications News*. Information Gatekeepers Inc. 8-9 (http://books.google.com/books?id=LN_Zp7f15X0C&pg=PA9&dq="Builders+Square"+"San+Antonio"&hl=en&ei=ezFHTKupH8LflgfV_720BA&sa=X&oi=book_result&ct=result&resnum=7&ved=0CEgQ6AEwBg#v=onepage&q="Builders Square" "San Antonio"&f=false). Retrieved from Google Books on July 21, 2010. ISSN 1079-2937.
[31] "Welcome to the 2009 U.S. Army All American Bowl" (http://www.usarmyallamericanbowl.com/). Usarmyallamericanbowl.com. . Retrieved 2010-06-30.
[32] Football: Cowboys returning to S.A. in '07 (http://www.mysanantonio.com/sports/football/nfl/cowboys/stories/MYSA040106.1C.FBNcowboys.alamodome.7ea018dc.html), *San Antonio Express-News*, April 1, 2006.
[33] Football: Cowboys' Jones backs S.A. team (http://www.mysanantonio.com/sports/football/nfl/stories/MYSA050506.3D.FBNcowboys.jones.c71335d.html), *San Antonio Express-News*, May 5, 2006.
[34] "New Expansion Teams" (http://web.archive.org/web/20080403084937/http://npsl.myeliteclub.com/LoadPage.aspx?iPage=24-48). Npsl.myeliteclub.com. Archived from the original (http://npsl.myeliteclub.com/LoadPage.aspx?iPage=24-48) on April 3, 2008. . Retrieved 2010-06-30.
[35] "City of San Antonio | Official Web Site - City Council" (http://www.sanantonio.gov/council/). Sanantonio.gov. . Retrieved 2010-06-30.
[36] http://www.sanantonio.gov/planning/pdf/GIS/map_download/0702GG24.pdf
[37] Texas Local Government Code section 212.003 (http://www.statutes.legis.state.tx.us/Docs/LG/htm/LG.212.htm#212.003), Extension of Rules to Extraterritorial Jurisdiction
[38] Extraterritorial Jurisdiction Boundary (PDF) (http://www.sanantonio.gov/planning/pdf/GIS/map_download/0607GT09.pdf), City of San Antonio Planning Department. July 28, 2006.
[39] San Antonio Master Plan (http://www.salsa.net/aiasa/sa-mastp.html), Public Studio (San Antonio Chapter American Institute of Architects). Retrieved January 7, 2007.
[40] San Antonio Trends, Challenges, and Opportunities (PowerPoint) (http://www.sanantonio.gov/planning/powerpoint/Growth_Trends_092506.pps), City of San Antonio Planning Department. Retrieved January 7, 2007.
[41] Three-year annexation plan (PDF) (http://www.sanantonio.gov/planning/pdf/Comprehensive/three_yr_plan/Three_Yr_Map_01_05_06.pdf), City of San Antonio Planning Department, January 6, 2006.
[42] San Antonio agrees to release ETJ to Schertz (http://www.mysanantonio.com/community/northeast/San_Antonio_agrees_to_release_ETJ_to_Schertz.html)
[43] MySA.com: Public Safety (http://www.mysanantonio.com/news/crime/stories/MYSA031107.01A.Fireresponsetimes.370d0e6.html)
[44] " Parole Division Region IV (http://www.tdcj.state.tx.us/parole/parole-directory/paroledir-rgnldisparoff4.htm)." Texas Department of Criminal Justice. Retrieved on May 21, 2010.

[45] " San Antonio District Office (http://www.dot.state.tx.us/local_information/san_antonio_district/)." Texas Department of Transportation. Retrieved on January 11, 2010.
[46] " Post Office Location - SAN ANTONIO (http://usps.whitepages.com/service/post_office/san-antonio-10410-perrin-beitel-rd-san-antonio-tx-1435860)." United States Postal Service. Retrieved on May 22, 2010.
[47] VIA Metropolitan Transit - Communications (http://viainfo.net/Communications/ViewArticle.aspx?ArticleId=1558)
[48] "VIA Metropolitan Transit" (http://www.viainfo.net/). .
[49] VIA Primo www.viabrt.net
[50] Lone Star Rail District www.lonestarrail.com
[51] "Amtrak's Texas Eagle | Welcome aboard!" (http://www.texaseagle.com/home.htm). Texaseagle.com. . Retrieved 2010-06-30.
[52] "Routes - California" (http://www.amtrak.com/servlet/ContentServer?pagename=Amtrak/am2Route/Horizontal_Route_Page&c=am2Route&cid=1081442673803&ssid=132). Amtrak. . Retrieved 2010-06-30.
[53] "Sunset Station San Antonio near the Convention Center, Alamo and River Walk Hotels" (http://www.sunset-station.com/). Sunset-station.com. . Retrieved 2010-06-30.
[54] Texas Department of Transportation. "Highway Designation File - State Highway Loop No. 345" (http://www.dot.state.tx.us/tpp/hwy/SL/SL0345.htm). .
[55] Texas Department of Transportation. "Highway Designation File - State Highway Loop No. 368" (http://www.dot.state.tx.us/tpp/hwy/SL/SL0368.htm). .
[56] Texas Department of Transportation. "Highway Designation File - State Highway Loop No. 353" (http://www.dot.state.tx.us/tpp/hwy/SL/SL0353.htm). .
[57] City of San Antonio | Official Web Site - San Antonio Bikes (http://www.sanantonio.gov/oep/sabikes/bicycleMP.aspx)
[58] Alamo City named bike-friendly city - San Antonio Business Journal (http://sanantonio.bizjournals.com/sanantonio/stories/2010/09/13/daily16.html)
[59] News Release - Bike Share Program (http://www.ci.sat.tx.us/news/NewsReleases/nr10bikeshare.asp?res=1600&ver=true)
[60] Bicycling proposals gear up (http://www.mysanantonio.com/news/politics/bicycling_proposals_gear_up_96533734.html?c=y&page=1#storytop)
[61] "2011 City and Neighborhood Rankings" (http://www.walkscore.com/rankings/cities/). Walk Score. 2011. . Retrieved Aug 28, 2011.
[62] MySA.com: Express-News About Us (http://www2.mysanantonio.com/aboutus/expressnews/)
[63] Designated Market Areas (http://www.nielsenmedia.com/DMAs.html), Nielson Media Research.
[64] http://www.210TV.com
[65] http://www.sainternationalrelations.org/sister-cities-program.html
[66] "Mayor announces Chennai, India Sister City Agreement" (http://www.sanantonio.gov/news/NewsMayorCouncil/nrChennaiSisterCity.asp?res=1280&ver=true). Sanantonio.gov. 2008-02-28. . Retrieved 2010-06-30.
[67] http://www.gsaccc.org/content/view/137/98/
[68] http://www.gsaccc.org/content/view/137/98/
[69] http://www.jta.org/news/article/2011/07/14/3088550/texas-mayor-signs-agreements-during-israel-trip

External links

- City of San Antonio (http://www.sanantonio.gov/)
- San Antonio Convention & Visitors Bureau (http://www.visitsanantonio.com/)
- San Antonio travel guide from Wikitravel
- San Antonio Neighborhood information (http://www.sanantoniohomes.com/neighborhoods.html)
- San Antonio International Airport (http://www.sanantonio-airport.com/)
- San Antonio area parks (http://www.wildtexas.com/parks/results.php?nearby_cities=San+Antonio)
- South and West Texas, a National Park Service *Discover Our Shared Heritage* Travel Itinerary (http://www.nps.gov/history/nr/travel/tx/)
- *San Antonio Missions: Spanish Influence in Texas,* a National Park Service Teaching with Historic Places (TwHP) lesson plan (http://www.nps.gov/history/NR/twhp/wwwlps/lessons/2sanantonio/2sanantonio.htm)
- San Antonio (http://www.tshaonline.org/handbook/online/articles/SS/hds2.html) from the *Handbook of Texas Online*
- Census quickfacts (http://quickfacts.census.gov/qfd/states/48/4865000.html)
- San Antonio City Data (http://www.city-data.com/city/San-Antonio-Texas.html)
- San Antonio Housing Statistics (http://san-antonio.housealmanac.com/)
- Port San Antonio (http://www.portsanantonio.us/)
- Downtown San Antonio (http://www.downtownsa.org/)

- Greater San Antonio Chamber of Commerce (http://www.sachamber.org/)
- The University of Texas at San Antonio houses a collection (http://www.lib.utexas.edu/taro/utsa/00018/utsa-00018.html) of papers by John Kight that documents the history of mass transit in San Antonio.

South Texas

South Texas is a region of the U.S. state of Texas that lies roughly south of and including San Antonio. The southern and western boundary is the Rio Grande River, and to the east it is the Gulf of Mexico. The population of this region is about 3.7 million. The southern portion of this region is often referred to as the Rio Grande Valley. The eastern portion along the Gulf of Mexico is also referred to as the Coastal Bend.

San Antonio is the largest city in South Texas.

Boundaries

There is no defined northern boundary, although it is believed to be at the city of San Antonio and from an east to west line extending from the Rio Grande near Maverick County to the Gulf of Mexico, but turning southeast at or near Lavaca County, and continuing towards the Gulf of Mexico to separate it from East Texas and Southeast Texas. The Rio Grande serves as the western and southern boundaries and separates Texas from Mexico. The eastern portion of South Texas is bordered by the Gulf of Mexico.

Corpus Christi is the second largest city in South Texas.

Laredo is the third largest city in South Texas, and it is also the fastest growing city in South Texas. The San Agustin Cathedral was built during the Spanish Texas period.

Brownsville is the fourth largest city in South Texas.

McAllen is the fifth largest city in South Texas.

Padre Island is a popular beach destination.

Most populous cities

City	2010 Census Population[1]	County
San Antonio	1,327,407	Bexar County
Corpus Christi	305,215	Nueces County
Laredo	236,091	Webb County
Brownsville	175,023	Cameron County
McAllen	129,877	Hidalgo County
Edinburg	77,100	Hidalgo County
Mission	77,058	Hidalgo County
Pharr	70,400	Hidalgo County
Harlingen	66,849	Cameron County
Victoria	62,592	Victoria County
Weslaco	35,670	Hidalgo County
San Juan	33,856	Hidalgo County
Eagle Pass	26,248	Maverick County
Kingsville	26,213	Kleberg County
San Benito	24,250	Cameron County

Alice	19,104	Jim Wells County

Some people consider Houston to be in South Texas for several reasons. Numerous businesses in the Houston region contain 'South Texas' in their titles.[2] The South Texas College of Law is located in downtown Houston. The United States District Court for the Southern District of Texas includes the Houston division. And like South Texas, the city has a large Hispanic population. However, Houston is most accurately classified as being within Southeast Texas, a subregion of East Texas.

Counties

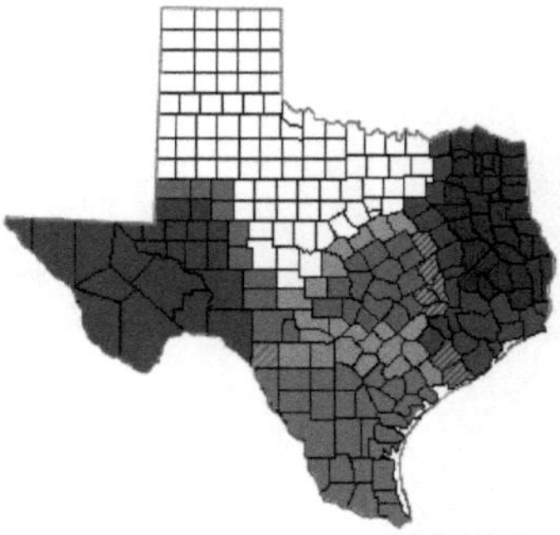

South Texas is depicted in Red and the northernmost counties in a lighter shade of red.

- Aransas
- Atascosa
- Bee
- Bexar
- Brooks
- Calhoun
- Cameron
- DeWitt
- Dimmit
- Duval
- Frio
- Goliad
- Gonzales
- Guadalupe
- Hidalgo
- Jackson
- Jim Hogg
- Jim Wells
- Karnes
- Kenedy
- Kinney
- Kleberg
- La Salle
- Lavaca
- Live Oak
- McMullen
- Matagorda
- Maverick
- Medina
- Nueces
- Refugio
- San Patricio
- Starr
- Uvalde
- Victoria
- Webb
- Wharton
- Willacy
- Wilson
- Zapata
- Zavala

Multicultural influences

South Texas is well-known for a strong Hispanic, primarily Mexican American and *Tejano* (the Spanish term for *Texan*) influence, due to its proximity to Mexico. Many Tejanos and Mexicans living in South Texas are descended from the Spanish and Sephardic Jewish-Converso settlers of Mexico. These families have resided in North America for hundreds of years. This migration occurred and has been ongoing since the late 16th century in New Mexico and the early 18th century in South Texas. The Treaty of Guadalupe Hidalgo in the 1840s, failed to secure land belonging to the Hispanic settlers. The disputed area was between the Nueces River south of San Antonio and Corpus Christi, the King Ranch, and the Rio Grande River. Not recognized by Mexico nor the United States, The Republic of the Rio Grande was established in this region in 1840, lasting less than a year. Laredo, Texas served as its capital.

The Rio Grande Valley area played a significant role in the Mexican War of Independence, Civil War, Texas Independence, Mexican-American War with many historical battle sites around the area. General Robert E. Lee made residence in Fort Ringold (Rio Grande City) during this time as a Colonel. President Zachary Taylor was a General of the Army at Fort Brown (Brownsville) during the Mexican-American War.

The Texas Rangers gained popularity for their actions in South Texas during the Mexican bandit raids and the late 19th century and early 20th century. On May 25, 1876, a band of forty Texas Rangers rode out of Laredo and headed north to the infamous Nueces Strip. Their mission was to find, kill or capture John King Fisher, leader of a band of cattle rustlers and cut-throats that had been terrorizing the area. The Rangers were members of a select group known as the Special Force. Led by the legendary Leander McNelly, the Special Force was tasked with bringing law and order to an area of South Texas that lay between Corpus Christi and the Mexican border.

Transportation

Air Travel

- San Antonio International Airport
- Corpus Christi International Airport
- Laredo International Airport
- Valley International Airport
- Victoria Regional Airport
- McAllen-Miller International Airport
- Brownsville/South Padre Island International Airport
- Alice International Airport
- South Texas International Airport at Edinburg
- Aransas County Airport[3]
- Kleberg County Airport
- Duval-Freer Airport
- Mustang Beach Airport
- San Jose Island Airport

Major Highways

Interstate Highways

- Interstate 10
- Interstate 35
- Interstate 37
- Interstate 69

United States Routes

- U.S. Highway 59
- U.S. Highway 77
- U.S. Highway 83
- U.S. Highway 87
- U.S. Highway 181
- U.S. Highway 281

Texas State Highways

- Texas Highway 4
- Texas Highway 16
- Texas Highway 44
- Texas Highway 107
- Texas Highway 255
- Texas Highway 336
- Texas Highway 359
- Texas Highway 361
- Texas Highway 495
- Texas Highway 141
- Texas Highway 290

International Bridges

Laredo

- Gateway to the Americas International Bridge
- Juarez-Lincoln International Bridge
- Texas-Mexican Railway International Bridge
- World Trade International Bridge
- Colombia-Solidarity International Bridge

Eagle Pass

- Eagle Pass-Piedras Negras International Bridge
- Camino Real International Bridge
- Union Pacific International Railroad Bridge

Brownsville

- Brownsville & Matamoros International Bridge
- Veteran's International Bridge
- Gateway International Bridge

Los Indios

- Free Trade International Bridge

Falcon Heights

- Lake Falcon Dam International Crossing

Hidalgo McAllen

- McAllen-Hidalgo-Reynosa International Bridge
- Anzalduas International Bridge

Pharr

- Pharr-Reynosa International Bridge

Progreso

- Progreso-Nuevo Progreso International Bridge

Rio Grande City

- Rio Grande City-Camargo International Bridge

Roma

- Roma-Ciudad Miguel Alemán International Bridge

Tourism

San Antonio

- The Alamo
- SeaWorld San Antonio
- Six Flags Fiesta Texas
- San Antonio River Walk
- San Antonio Zoo
- San Antonio Museum of Art
- San Antonio Stock Show & Rodeo

Corpus Christi

- Mirador de la Flor (Selena Memorial Statue)
- Texas State Aquarium
- USS Lexington Museum Ship
- Mustang Island & Mustang Island State Park
- Padre Island National Seashore near Corpus Christi
- Bayfest

Laredo

- San Agustin de Laredo Historic District
- Republic of the Rio Grande Capitol Building Museum
- Washington's Birthday Celebration festivities during January and February

Rio Grande Valley

- South Padre Island on Gulf Coast east of Brownsville
- Gladys Porter Zoo in Brownsville

Other

- King Ranch near Kingsville
- Aransas National Wildlife Refuge

San Antonio river walk

South Padre Island

SeaWorld San Antonio

The Alamo

Corpus Christi

USS Lexington floating museum in Corpus Christi

San Agustin Cathedral in Laredo's San Agustin de Laredo Historic District

Republic of the Rio Grande Capitol building is located in Laredo

Education

Colleges

- Alamo Community College District
  - San Antonio College
  - Palo Alto College
  - St. Philip's College
  - Northeast Lakeview College
  - Northwest Vista College
- Coastal Bend College
  - Alice Campus
  - Main Campus (Beeville)
  - Kingsville Campus
  - Pleasanton Campus
- Del Mar College
- Laredo Community College
  - Laredo Community College South Campus
- South Texas College
  - Main Campus, McAllen
  - Tech Campus, McAllen
  - Nursing and Allied Health Campus, McAllen
  - Mid-Valley Campus, Weslaco
  - Starr County Campus, Rio Grande City
- Texas State Technical College

Universities

Public universities

- Texas A&M International University (Laredo)
- Texas A&M University–Corpus Christi
- Texas A&M University–Kingsville (Texas A&I)
- Texas A&M University-San Antonio
- University of Houston–Victoria
- University of Texas at Brownsville
- University of Texas–Pan American
- University of Texas Health Science Center at San Antonio
- University of Texas at San Antonio

Private universities

- Our Lady of the Lake University
- St. Mary's University
- University of the Incarnate Word
- Trinity University
- Wayland Baptist University

Sports

The only major professional sports team in South Texas is the San Antonio Spurs in the NBA.

Team	Sport	League	Venue
San Antonio Spurs	Basketball	NBA	AT&T Center
San Antonio Silver Stars		WNBA	
Rio Grande Valley Vipers		NBA D-League	State Farm Arena
Corpus Christi Hammerheads	Arena Football	IFL	Central Pavilion Arena
Corpus Christi Hooks	Baseball	Texas League	Whataburger Field
San Antonio Missions			Nelson W. Wolff Municipal Stadium
Laredo Lemurs		AAIPB	Laredo Ballpark
McAllen Thunder		North American League	Fairgrounds Field
Edinburg Roadrunners			Edinburg Stadium
Rio Grande Valley WhiteWings			Harlingen Field
San Antonio Rampage	Ice hockey	American Hockey League	AT&T Center
Corpus Christi IceRays		North American Hockey League	American Bank Center
Laredo Bucks		Central Hockey League	Laredo Energy Arena
Rio Grande Valley Killer Bees			State Farm Arena
Laredo Heat	Soccer	PDL	TAMIU Soccer Complex
Rio Grande Valley Grandes			Valley View High School Stadium

Area codes

- 210 - San Antonio
- 361 - Corpus Christi, Alice, Victoria, Kingsville, Rockport
- 956 - Laredo, Brownsville, McAllen
- 830 - Eagle Pass, San Antonio
- 979 - only the southern half of this area is in South Texas

See also

- List of geographical regions in Texas
- List of Texas regions

References

[1] Census Fact Finder (http://factfinder.census.gov/home/saff/main.html?_lang=en)
[2] (http://maps.google.com/maps?f=q&hl=en&geocode=&q=south+texas+houston,+tx&mrt=yp&ie=UTF8&start=0&z=12)
[3] Aransas County Airport Website (http://www.krkp.com/) Aransas Co Airport Call Sign: RKP(U.S), KRKP(International)

Savings account

Savings accounts are accounts maintained by retail financial institutions that pay interest but cannot be used directly as money (for example, by writing a check). These accounts let customers set aside a portion of their liquid assets while earning a monetary return. For the bank, money in a savings account may not be callable immediately and therefore often does not incur a reserve requirement freeing up cash from the bank's vault to be lent out with interest.

The other major types of deposit account are transactional (checking) account, money market account, and time deposit.

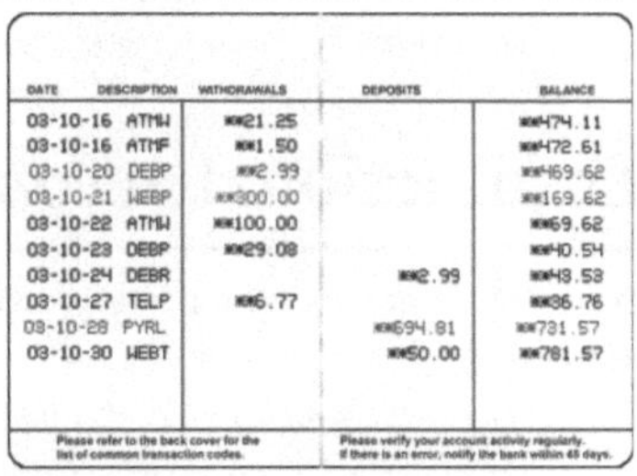

DATE	DESCRIPTION	WITHDRAWALS	DEPOSITS	BALANCE
03-10-16	ATMW	**21.25		**474.11
03-10-16	ATMF	**1.50		**472.61
03-10-20	DEBP	**2.99		**469.62
03-10-21	WEBP	**300.00		**169.62
03-10-22	ATMW	**100.00		**69.62
03-10-23	DEBP	**29.08		**40.54
03-10-24	DEBR		**2.99	**43.53
03-10-27	TELP	**6.77		**36.76
03-10-28	PYRL		**694.81	**731.57
03-10-30	WEBT		**50.00	**781.57

Please refer to the back cover for the list of common transaction codes.
Please verify your account activity regularly. If there is an error, notify the bank within 45 days.

A passbook, the traditional record of savings account transactions

Regulation

In the United States, under Regulation D, 12 CFR 204.2(d)(2), the term "savings deposit" includes a deposit or an account that meets the requirements of Sec. 204.2(d)(1) and from which, under the terms of the deposit contract or by practice of the depository institution, the depositor is permitted or authorized to make up to six transfers or withdrawals per month or statement cycle of at least four weeks. The depository institution may authorize up to three of these six transfers to be made by check, draft, debit card, or similar order drawn by the depositor and payable to third parties. There is no regulation limiting number of deposits, but some banks choose themselves to limit deposits.

Within most European countries, interest paid on deposit accounts is taxed at source. The high rates of some countries has led to the development of a significant offshore savings industry. The financial centres for either information on interest earned to be shared with EU tax authorities or for withholding tax to be deducted on interest paid on offshore accounts, because of concerns relating to potential tax evasion. Account holders must either pay the withholding tax or disclose account holder information to relevant tax authorities.[1]

Costs

Withdrawals from a savings account are occasionally costly and are sometimes much higher and more time-consuming than the same financial transaction being performed on a demand (current) account. However, most savings accounts do not limit withdrawals, unlike certificates of deposit. In the United States, violations of Regulation D often involve a service charge, or even a downgrade of the account to a checking account. With online accounts, the main penalty is the time required for the Automated Clearing House to transfer funds from the online account to a "brick and mortar" bank where it can be easily accessed. During the period between when funds are withdrawn from the online bank and transferred to the local bank, no interest is earned.

Online savings accounts

Some financial institutions offer online-only savings accounts. These usually pay higher interest rates and sometimes carry higher security restrictions.

References

[1] Budden, Robert; Cumbo, Josephine (7 July 2006). "Offshore investors beat EU directive to avoid tax" (http://www.ft.com/cms/s/ae51ab84-0d9f-11db-a385-0000779e2340.html). *Financial Times*. . Retrieved 28 November 2010.

External links

- Online Banking (http://www.dmoz.org//Business/Financial_Services/Banking_Services/Online_Banking/) at the Open Directory Project

Transactional account

A **transactional account** is a deposit account held at a bank or other financial institution, for the purpose of securely and quickly providing frequent access to funds on demand, through a variety of different channels.

Transactional accounts are meant neither for the purpose of earning interest nor for the purpose of savings, but for convenience of the business or personal client; hence they tend not to bear interest. Instead, a customer can deposit or withdraw any amount of money any number of times, subject to availability of funds.

Name

A transactional account is known as a **checking account** (or **chequing account**) in North America,[1] and as a **current account** or **cheque account** in the United Kingdom, Hong Kong and some other countries. Because money is available on demand it is also sometimes known as a **demand account** or **demand deposit account**.

History

In Holland in the early 1500s Amsterdam was a major trading and shipping city. In order to protect their large accumulations of cash, people began to depositing their money with "cashiers". These cashiers held the money for a fee. Competition drove cashiers to offer additional services including paying out money to any person bearing a written order from a depositor to do so. They kept the note as proof of payment.

This idea spread to other countries including England, and the English colonies in North America, where land owners in Boston in 1681 mortgaged their land to cashiers which would provide an account against which they could write checks.

In the eighteenth century in England preprinted checks, serial numbers, and the very word "cheque" appeared. By the late eighteenth century, the difficulty of clearing checks (sending them from one bank to another for collection) gave rise to the development of clearing houses.

Features and access

All transactional accounts offer itemized lists of all financial transactions, either through a bank statement or a passbook. A transactional account allows the account holder to make or receive payments by:

- ATM cards (withdraw cash at any Automated Teller Machine)
- debit card (cashless direct payment at a store or merchant)
- cash money (coins and banknotes)
- cheque and money order (paper instruction to pay)
- direct debit (pre-authorized debit)
- Electronic funds transfers (transfer funds electronically to another account)
- giro (funds transfer, direct deposit)
- standing order (automatic funds transfer)
- SWIFT: International account to account transfer.
- Online banking (transfer funds directly to another person via internet banking facility)

Country specific

Certain modes of payment are country-specific:

- In the United Kingdom, BACS offers giros that clear in a matter of days while CHAPS is done on the same day.
- Canada has an Email Money Transfer service
- The United States offers e-checks.
- In India, NEFT and RTGS services are available to

The cheque is the traditional mode of payment for a transactional account.

Access

Branch networks

An Automated Teller Machine (ATM)

This refers to the practice of maintaining physical locations where customers can receive a wide array of banking and financial services, such locations are described as branches. They may provide access to a combination of cash machines, telephone banking, counter services and financial advice.

Overdrafts

In North America, overdraft protection is an optional feature of a chequing account. An account holder may either apply for a permanent one, or the financial institution may, at its sole discretion, provide a temporary overdraft on an ad-hoc basis.

Interest

Formerly, in the United States, Regulation Q (12 CFR 217) and the Banking Acts of 1933 and 1935 (12 USC 371a) prohibited a member of the Federal Reserve system from paying interest on chequing accounts. Historically, this restriction was frequently circumvented by either creating an account type such as a Negotiable Order of Withdrawal account (NOW account) which is legally not a chequing account or by offering interest paying chequing through a bank which is not a member of the Federal Reserve system. The Dodd-Frank Wall Street Reform and Consumer Protection Act, however, passed by Congress and signed into law by President Obama on July 21, 2010, repealed the statutes that prohibit interest-bearing transactional accounts, effectively repealing Regulation Q (Pub. L. 111-203, Section 627). The repeal took effect on July 21, 2011. Since that date, financial institutions have been permitted, but not required, to offer interest-bearing transactional accounts.

High-yield checking accounts

High-interest NOW accounts have become prevalent throughout the industry. They pay a higher interest rate than typical NOW accounts and frequently function as loss-leaders to drive relationship banking.

In 2003, banks and credit unions began to establish maximum balance accounts, which pay a premium rate up to a specified cap and a lower rate on balances above the cap. This counter-traditional trend (banks had typically established minimum account balances rather than maximum account balances) developed as a way to allow financial institutions to attract multiple customer relationships while limiting the interest expense associated with each account.

The first maximum balance, high-interest chequing account was offered in 2003 by a small community bank in New Mexico, Pioneer Bank. In 2004 and 2005, several community banks in West Texas adopted the idea, and a 3rd party vendor, BancVue, combined the maximum-balance concept with the idea of a higher yield for customers who adopt specific cost-savings behaviors, as a "Reward" Checking account.

Other imitators rapidly followed. By 2010, over 1.5 million REWARDChecking(r) accounts had been opened at BancVue's clients alone.[2]

The repeal of Regulation Q, which previously prohibited the payment of interest on standard transactional accounts, took effect too recently for it to have shown a major impact on banking practices. It is likely, however, that as time progresses the popularity of these alternative "checking" accounts will decline as clients opt for the less restrictive rules governing standard transactional accounts.

Internet banking

Internet or Online banking describes the use of a bank's secure website to view balances and statements, perform transactions and payments, and various other facilities. This can be very useful, especially for banking outside bank hours and banking from anywhere where internet access is available. Since the internet revolution most retail banking institutions offer access to current accounts via online banking.

Telephone banking

Telephone banking is the term applied to specific provision of banking services over the telephone. In many cases such calls are to a call centre or automated service, although some institutions continue to answer such calls in their branches. Often call centre opening times are considerably longer than branches, and some firms provide these services on a 24 hour basis.

Overdrafts

An overdraft occurs when withdrawals from a bank account exceed the available balance. This gives the account a negative balance and in effect means the account provider is providing credit. If there is a prior agreement with the account provider for an overdraft facility, and the amount overdrawn is within this authorised overdraft, then interest is normally charged at the agreed rate. If the balance exceeds the agreed facility then fees may be charged and a higher interest rate might apply.

Cost

The policy of charging a fee for doing financial transactions depends on a variety of factors, including the country and its overall interest rates for lending and for saving, as well as the size of the financial institution and the number of channels of access it offers. This is why operating few or no branches can afford to offer low-cost or free banking, and why, in some countries, transaction fees do not exist, but extremely high lending rates are the normal.

Financial transaction fees may be charged either per item or for a flat rate covering a certain number of transactions. Often, youths, students, senior citizens or high-valued customers do not pay fees for basic financial transactions. Some will offer free transactions for maintaining a very high average balance in their account. Other service charges are applicable for overdraft, non-sufficient funds, the use of an external interbank network, etc. In countries where there are no service charges for transaction fees, there are, on the other hand, other recurring service charges such as a debit card annual fee.

Interest

Unlike savings accounts, for which the primary reason for depositing money is to generate interest, the main function of a transactional account is transactional. Therefore, most providers either pay no interest or pay a low level of interest on credit balances.

Current accounts

A current account is the form of transactional account found in the United Kingdom and other countries with a UK banking heritage; a current account offers various flexible payment methods to allow customers to distribute money directly to others. Most current accounts come with a cheque book and offer the facility to arrange standing orders, direct debits and payment via a debit card. Current accounts may also allow borrowing via an overdraft facility.

Lending

Current accounts have two different ways in which money can be lent: overdraft and offset mortgage.

Overdraft

In the UK, virtually all current accounts offer a pre-agreed overdraft facility the size of which is based upon affordability and credit history. This overdraft facility can be used at any time without consulting the bank and can be maintained indefinitely (subject to ad-hoc reviews). Although an overdraft facility may be authorised, technically the money is repayable on demand by the bank. In reality this is a rare occurrence as the overdrafts are profitable for the bank and expensive for the customer.

Offset mortgage

An offset mortgage was a type of mortgage common in the United Kingdom used for the purchase of domestic property, the key principle is the reduction of interest charged by "offsetting" a credit balance against the mortgage debt. This can be achieved via one of two methods either lenders provide a single account for all transactions (often referred to as a current account mortgage) or they make multiple accounts available which allow the borrowers to notionally split their money according to purpose whilst all accounts are offset each day against the mortgage debt.

Interest

In the UK some online banks offer rates as high as many savings accounts along with free banking (no charges for transactions) as institutions which offer centralised services (telephone, internet or postal based) tend to pay higher levels of interest. The same holds true for banks within the EURO currency zone.

See also

Transaction related

- Collection item
- Error account a necessity for auditing transaction accounts
- Demand draft
- Transaction deposit

Account type related

- Current account mortgage
- Negotiable Order of Withdrawal account
- Personal account
- Savings account

Notes

[1] U.S. and Canadian spelling, respectively; see further at Etymology and spelling.
[2] Media.sugarcrm.com (http://media.sugarcrm.com/case_studies/BancVue.pdf)

Loan

A **loan** is a type of debt. Like all debt instruments, a loan entails the redistribution of financial assets over time, between the lender and the borrower.

In a loan, the borrower initially receives or *borrows* an amount of money, called the *principal*, from the lender, and is obligated to *pay back* or *repay* an equal amount of money to the lender at a later time. Typically, the money is paid back in regular *installments*, or partial repayments; in an annuity, each installment is the same amount.

The loan is generally provided at a cost, referred to as interest on the debt, which provides an incentive for the lender to engage in the loan. In a legal loan, each of these obligations and restrictions is enforced by contract, which can also place the borrower under additional restrictions known as loan covenants. Although this article focuses on monetary loans, in practice any material object might be lent.

Acting as a provider of loans is one of the principal tasks for financial institutions. For other institutions, issuing of debt contracts such as bonds is a typical source of funding.

Types of loans

Secured

A secured loan is a loan in which the borrower pledges some asset (e.g. a car or property) as collateral for the loan.

A subsidized loan is a loan that will not gain interest before you begin to pay it. It is known to be used at multiple colleges.

An unsubsidized loan is a loan that gains interest the day of disbursement.

A mortgage loan is a very common type of debt instrument, used by many individuals to purchase housing. In this arrangement, the money is used to purchase the property. The financial institution, however, is given security — a lien on the title to the house — until the mortgage is paid off in full. If the borrower defaults on the loan, the bank would have the legal right to repossess the house and sell it, to recover sums owing to it.

In some instances, a loan taken out to purchase a new or used car may be secured by the car, in much the same way as a mortgage is secured by housing. The duration of the loan period is considerably shorter — often corresponding to the useful life of the car. There are two types of auto loans, direct and indirect. A direct auto loan is where a bank gives the loan directly to a consumer. An indirect auto loan is where a car dealership acts as an intermediary between the bank or financial institution and the consumer.

A type of loan especially used in limited partnership agreements is the recourse note.

A stock hedge loan is a special type of securities lending whereby the stock of a borrower is hedged by the lender against loss, using options or other hedging strategies to reduce lender risk.

A pre-settlement loan is a non-recourse debt, this is when a monetary loan is given based on the merit and awardable amount in a lawsuit case. Only certain types of lawsuit cases are eligible for a pre-settlement loan. This is considered a secured non-recourse debt because if the case reaches a verdict in favor of the defendant the loan is forgiven.

Unsecured

Unsecured loans are monetary loans that are not secured against the borrower's assets. These may be available from financial institutions under many different guises or marketing packages:

- credit card debt
- personal loans
- bank overdrafts
- credit facilities or lines of credit
- corporate bonds (may be secured or unsecured)

The interest rates applicable to these different forms may vary depending on the lender and the borrower. These may or may not be regulated by law. In the United Kingdom, when applied to individuals, these may come under the Consumer Credit Act 1974.

Demand

Demand loans are short term loans (typically no more than 180 days)[1] that are atypical in that they do not have fixed dates for repayment and carry a floating interest rate which varies according to the prime rate. They can be "called" for repayment by the lending institution at any time. Demand loans may be unsecured or secured.

Target markets

Personal or commercial

Loans can also be subcategorized according to whether the debtor is an individual person (consumer) or a business. Common personal loans include mortgage loans, car loans, home equity lines of credit, credit cards, installment loans and payday loans. The credit score of the borrower is a major component in and underwriting and interest rates (APR) of these loans. The monthly payments of personal loans can be decreased by selecting longer payment terms, but overall interest paid increases as well. For car loans in the U.S., the average term was about 60 months in 2009.[2]

Loans to businesses are similar to the above, but also include commercial mortgages and corporate bonds. Underwriting is not based upon credit score but rather credit rating.

Loan payment

The most typical loan payment type is the fully amortizing payment in which each monthly rate has the same value overtime.[3]

The fixed monthly payment **P** for a loan of **L** for **n** months and a monthly interest rate **c** is: [4]

Abuses in lending

Predatory lending is one form of abuse in the granting of loans. It usually involves granting a loan in order to put the borrower in a position that one can gain advantage over him or her. Where the moneylender is not authorized, they could be considered a loan shark.

Usury is a different form of abuse, where the lender charges excessive interest. In different time periods and cultures the acceptable interest rate has varied, from no interest at all to unlimited interest rates. Credit card companies in some countries have been accused by consumer organisations of lending at usurious interest rates and making money out of frivolous "extra charges".[5]

Abuses can also take place in the form of the customer abusing the lender by not repaying the loan or with an intent to defraud the lender.

United States taxes

Most of the basic rules governing how loans are handled for tax purposes in the United States are codified by both Congress (the Internal Revenue Code) and the Treasury Department (Treasury Regulations — another set of rules that interpret the Internal Revenue Code).[6] Yet such rules are universally accepted.[7]

1. **A loan is not gross income to the borrower.**[8] Since the borrower has the obligation to repay the loan, the borrower has no accession to wealth.[9]

2. **The lender may not deduct (from own gross income) the amount of the loan.**[10] The rationale here is that one asset (the cash) has been converted into a different asset (a promise of repayment).[11] Deductions are not typically available when an outlay serves to create a new or different asset.[12]

3. **The amount paid to satisfy the loan obligation is not deductible (from own gross income) by the borrower.**[13]

4. **Repayment of the loan is not gross income to the lender.**[14] In effect, the promise of repayment is converted back to cash, with no accession to wealth by the lender.[15]

5. **Interest paid to the lender is included in the lender's gross income.**[16] Interest paid represents compensation for the use of the lender's money or property and thus represents profit or an accession to wealth to the lender.[17] Interest income can be attributed to lenders even if the lender doesn't charge a minimum amount of interest.[18]

6. **Interest paid to the lender may be deductible by the borrower.**[19] In general, interest paid in connection with the borrower's business activity is deductible, while interest paid on personal loans are not deductible.[20] The major exception here is interest paid on a home mortgage.[21]

Income from discharge of indebtedness

Although a loan does not start out as income to the borrower, it becomes income to the borrower if the borrower is discharged of indebtedness. [22] **Thus, if a debt is discharged, then the borrower essentially has received income equal to the amount of the indebtedness. The Internal Revenue Code lists "Income from Discharge of Indebtedness" in Section 61(a)(12) as a source of gross income.**

Example: X owes Y $50,000. If Y discharges the indebtedness, then X no longer owes Y $50,000. For purposes of calculating income, this should be treated the same way as if Y gave X $50,000.

For a more detailed description of the "discharge of indebtedness", look at Section 108 (Cancellation of Debt (COD) Income) of the Internal Revenue Code.[23]

See also

- Finance, Personal finance, Settlement (finance)
- Debt, Consumer debt, Debt consolidation, Government debt
- Bank, Fractional-reserve banking, Building society
- Annual percentage rate (a.k.a. Effective annual rate)
- Default (finance)
- Interest-only loan, Negative amortization, PIK loan
- Loan guarantee
- Loan sale
- Payday loan
- Refund Anticipation Loan
- Student loan
- Syndicated loan
- Title loan

US specific:

- FAFSA
- Federal student loan consolidation
- Federal Perkins Loan
- George D. Sax and the Exchange National Bank of Chicago - Innovation of instant loans
- Stafford loan
- Student loan default

References

[1] Signoriello, Vincent J. (1991), *Commercial Loan Practices and Operations*, ISBN 9781555201340

[2] Bird C. Car Loans: How Long Should They Be? (http://www.cars.com/go/advice/Story.jsp?section=fin&story=car-loans-how-long&subject=car-loan-tips&referer=&aff=national). Cars.com.

[3] Guttentag, Jack (October 6, 2007). "The Math Behind Your Home Loan" (http://www.washingtonpost.com/wp-dyn/content/article/2007/10/05/AR2007100501165.html). *The Washington Post*. . Retrieved May 11, 2010.

[4] http://www.mtgprofessor.com/formulas.htm

[5] Credit card holders pay Rs 6,000 cr 'extra' (http://www.financialexpress.com/latest_full_story.php?content_id=163028) May 3, 2007

[6] Samuel A. Donaldson, Federal Income Taxation of Individuals: Cases, Problems and Materials, 2nd Ed. 111 (2007).

[7] *Id.*

[8] *Id.*

[9] *Id. See Commissioner v. Glenshaw Glass Co.*, 348 U.S. 426 (1955)(giving the three-prong standard for what is "income" for tax purposes: (1) accession to wealth, (2) clearly realized, (3) over which the taxpayer has complete dominion).

[10] Donaldson, at 111.

[11] *Id.*

[12] *Id.*

[13] *Id.*

[14] *Id.*

[15] *Id.*

[16] *Id.*; 26 U.S.C. 61(a)(4)(2007).

[17] *Id.*

[18] *Id. at 112.*

[19] *Id.*

[20] *Id.*

[21] *Id.*

[22] *Id.*; 26 U.S.C. 61(a)(12)(2007).

[23] *Id.*; 26 U.S.C. 108(2007).

Mortgage loan

A **mortgage loan** is a loan secured by real property through the use of a mortgage note which evidences the existence of the loan and the encumbrance of that realty through the granting of a mortgage which secures the loan. However, the word *mortgage* alone, in everyday usage, is most often used to mean *mortgage loan*.

A home buyer or builder can obtain financing (a loan) either to purchase or secure against the property from a financial institution, such as a bank, either directly or indirectly through intermediaries. Features of mortgage loans such as the size of the loan, maturity of the loan, interest rate, method of paying off the loan, and other characteristics can vary considerably.

In many jurisdictions, though not all (Bali, Indonesia being one exception[1]), it is normal for home purchases to be funded by a mortgage loan. Few individuals have enough savings or liquid funds to enable them to purchase property outright. In countries where the demand for home ownership is highest, strong domestic markets have developed.

The word *mortgage* is a Law French term meaning "dead pledge," apparently meaning that the pledge ends (dies) either when the obligation is fulfilled or the property is taken through foreclosure.[2]

Mortgage loan basics

Basic concepts and legal regulation

According to Anglo-American property law, a mortgage occurs when an owner (usually of a fee simple interest in realty) pledges his interest (right to the property) as security or collateral for a loan. Therefore, a mortgage is an encumbrance (limitation) on the right to the property just as an easement would be, but because most mortgages occur as a condition for new loan money, the word *mortgage* has become the generic term for a loan secured by such real property.[3]

As with other types of loans, mortgages have an interest rate and are scheduled to amortize over a set period of time, typically 30 years. All types of real property can be, and usually are, secured with a mortgage and bear an interest rate that is supposed to reflect the lender's risk.

Mortgage lending is the primary mechanism used in many countries to finance private ownership of residential and commercial property (see commercial mortgages). Although the terminology and precise forms will differ from country to country, the basic components tend to be similar:

- Property: the physical residence being financed. The exact form of ownership will vary from country to country, and may restrict the types of lending that are possible.
- Mortgage: the security interest of the lender in the property, which may entail restrictions on the use or disposal of the property. Restrictions may include requirements to purchase home insurance and mortgage insurance, or pay off outstanding debt before selling the property.
- Borrower: the person borrowing who either has or is creating an ownership interest in the property.
- Lender: any lender, but usually a bank or other financial institution. Lenders may also be investors who own an interest in the mortgage through a mortgage-backed security. In such a situation, the initial lender is known as the mortgage originator, which then packages and sells the loan to investors. The payments from the borrower are thereafter collected by a loan servicer.[4]
- Principal: the original size of the loan, which may or may not include certain other costs; as any principal is repaid, the principal will go down in size.
- Interest: a financial charge for use of the lender's money.
- Foreclosure or repossession: the possibility that the lender has to foreclose, repossess or seize the property under certain circumstances is essential to a mortgage loan; without this aspect, the loan is arguably no different from any other type of loan.

Many other specific characteristics are common to many markets, but the above are the essential features. Governments usually regulate many aspects of mortgage lending, either directly (through legal requirements, for example) or indirectly (through regulation of the participants or the financial markets, such as the banking industry), and often through state intervention (direct lending by the government, by state-owned banks, or sponsorship of various entities). Other aspects that define a specific mortgage market may be regional, historical, or driven by specific characteristics of the legal or financial system.

Mortgage loans are generally structured as long-term loans, the periodic payments for which are similar to an annuity and calculated according to the time value of money formulae. The most basic arrangement would require a fixed monthly payment over a period of ten to thirty years, depending on local conditions. Over this period the principal component of the loan (the original loan) would be slowly paid down through amortization. In practice, many variants are possible and common worldwide and within each country.

Lenders provide funds against property to earn interest income, and generally borrow these funds themselves (for example, by taking deposits or issuing bonds). The price at which the lenders borrow money therefore affects the cost of borrowing. Lenders may also, in many countries, sell the mortgage loan to other parties who are interested in receiving the stream of cash payments from the borrower, often in the form of a security (by means of a securitization).

Mortgage lending will also take into account the (perceived) riskiness of the mortgage loan, that is, the likelihood that the funds will be repaid (usually considered a function of the creditworthiness of the borrower); that if they are not repaid, the lender will be able to foreclose and recoup some or all of its original capital; and the financial, interest rate risk and time delays that may be involved in certain circumstances.

Mortgage loan types

There are many types of mortgages used worldwide, but several factors broadly define the characteristics of the mortgage. All of these may be subject to local regulation and legal requirements.

- Interest: interest may be fixed for the life of the loan or variable, and change at certain pre-defined periods; the interest rate can also, of course, be higher or lower.
- Term: mortgage loans generally have a maximum term, that is, the number of years after which an amortizing loan will be repaid. Some mortgage loans may have no amortization, or require full repayment of any remaining balance at a certain date, or even negative amortization.
- Payment amount and frequency: the amount paid per period and the frequency of payments; in some cases, the amount paid per period may change or the borrower may have the option to increase or decrease the amount paid.
- Prepayment: some types of mortgages may limit or restrict prepayment of all or a portion of the loan, or require payment of a penalty to the lender for prepayment.

The two basic types of amortized loans are the fixed rate mortgage (FRM) and adjustable-rate mortgage (ARM) (also known as a floating rate or variable rate mortgage). In many countries (such as the United States), floating rate mortgages are the norm and will simply be referred to as mortgages. Combinations of fixed and floating rate are also common, whereby a mortgage loan will have a fixed rate for some period, and vary after the end of that period.

- In a fixed rate mortgage, the interest rate, and hence periodic payment, remains fixed for the life (or term) of the loan. Therefore the payment is fixed, although ancillary costs (such as property taxes and insurance) can and do change. For a fixed rate mortgage, payments for principal and interest should not change over the life of the loan,
- In an adjustable rate mortgage, the interest rate is generally fixed for a period of time, after which it will periodically (for example, annually or monthly) adjust up or down to some market index. Adjustable rates transfer part of the interest rate risk from the lender to the borrower, and thus are widely used where fixed rate funding is difficult to obtain or prohibitively expensive. Since the risk is transferred to the borrower, the initial interest rate may be from 0.5% to 2% lower than the average 30-year fixed rate; the size of the price differential will be related to debt market conditions, including the yield curve.

The charge to the borrower depends upon the credit risk in addition to the interest rate risk. The mortgage origination and underwriting process involves checking credit scores, debt-to-income, downpayments, and assets. Jumbo mortgages and subprime lending are not supported by government guarantees and face higher interest rates. Other innovations described below can affect the rates as well.

Mortgage underwriting

Loan to value and downpayments

Upon making a mortgage loan for the purchase of a property, lenders usually require that the borrower make a downpayment; that is, contribute a portion of the cost of the property. This downpayment may be expressed as a portion of the value of the property (see below for a definition of this term). The loan to value ratio (or LTV) is the size of the loan against the value of the property. Therefore, a mortgage loan in which the purchaser has made a downpayment of 20% has a loan to value ratio of 80%. For loans made against properties that the borrower already owns, the loan to value ratio will be imputed against the estimated value of the property.

The loan to value ratio is considered an important indicator of the riskiness of a mortgage loan: the higher the LTV, the higher the risk that the value of the property (in case of foreclosure) will be insufficient to cover the remaining principal of the loan.

Value: appraised, estimated, and actual

Since the value of the property is an important factor in understanding the risk of the loan, determining the value is a key factor in mortgage lending. The value may be determined in various ways, but the most common are:

1. Actual or transaction value: this is usually taken to be the purchase price of the property. If the property is not being purchased at the time of borrowing, this information may not be available.
2. Appraised or surveyed value: in most jurisdictions, some form of appraisal of the value by a licensed professional is common. There is often a requirement for the lender to obtain an official appraisal.
3. Estimated value: lenders or other parties may use their own internal estimates, particularly in jurisdictions where no official appraisal procedure exists, but also in some other circumstances.

Payment and debt ratios

In most countries, a number of more or less standard measures of creditworthiness may be used. Common measures include payment to income (mortgage payments as a percentage of gross or net income); debt to income (all debt payments, including mortgage payments, as a percentage of income); and various net worth measures. In many countries, credit scores are used in lieu of or to supplement these measures. There will also be requirements for documentation of the creditworthiness, such as income tax returns, pay stubs, etc; the specifics will vary from location to location.

Some lenders may also require a potential borrower have one or more months of "reserve assets" available. In other words, the borrower may be required to show the availability of enough assets to pay for the housing costs (including mortgage, taxes, etc.) for a period of time in the event of the job loss or other loss of income.

Many countries have lower requirements for certain borrowers, or "no-doc" / "low-doc" lending standards that may be acceptable in certain circumstances.

Standard or conforming mortgages

Many countries have a notion of standard or conforming mortgages that define a perceived acceptable level of risk, which may be formal or informal, and may be reinforced by laws, government intervention, or market practice. For example, a standard mortgage may be considered to be one with no more than 70-80% LTV and no more than one-third of gross income going to mortgage debt.

A standard or conforming mortgage is a key concept as it often defines whether or not the mortgage can be easily sold or securitized, or, if non-standard, may affect the price at which it may be sold. In the United States, a conforming mortgage is one which meets the established rules and procedures of the two major government-sponsored entities in the housing finance market (including some legal requirements). In contrast, lenders who decide to make nonconforming loans are exercising a higher risk tolerance and do so knowing that they face more challenge in reselling the loan. Many countries have similar concepts or agencies that define what are "standard" mortgages. Regulated lenders (such as banks) may be subject to limits or higher risk weightings for non-standard mortgages. For example, banks and mortgage brokerages in Canada face restrictions on lending more than 80% of the property value; beyond this level, mortgage insurance is generally required.[5]

Foreign currency mortgage

In some countries with currencies that tend to depreciate, foreign currency mortgages are common, enabling lenders to lend in a stable foreign currency, whilst the borrower takes on the currency risk that the currency will depreciate and they will therefore need to convert higher amounts of the domestic currency to repay the loan.

Repaying the mortgage

In addition to the two standard means of setting the *cost* of a mortgage loan (fixed at a set interest rate for the term, or variable relative to market interest rates), there are variations in *how* that cost is paid, and how the loan itself is repaid. Repayment depends on locality, tax laws and prevailing culture. There are also various mortgage repayment structures to suit different types of borrower.

Capital and interest

The most common way to repay a secured mortgage loan is to make regular payments of the capital (also called the principal) and interest over a set term.[6] This is commonly referred to as (self) **amortization** in the U.S. and as a **repayment mortgage** in the UK. A mortgage is a form of annuity (from the perspective of the lender), and the calculation of the periodic payments is based on the time value of money formulas. Certain details may be specific to different locations: interest may be calculated on the basis of a 360-day year, for example; interest may be compounded daily, yearly, or semi-annually; prepayment penalties may apply; and other factors. There may be legal restrictions on certain matters, and consumer protection laws may specify or prohibit certain practices.

Depending on the size of the loan and the prevailing practice in the country the term may be short (10 years) or long (50 years plus). In the UK and U.S., 25 to 30 years is the usual maximum term (although shorter periods, such as 15-year mortgage loans, are common). Mortgage payments, which are typically made monthly, contain a capital (repayment of the principal) and an interest element. The amount of capital included in each payment varies throughout the term of the mortgage. In the early years the repayments are largely interest and a small part capital. Towards the end of the mortgage the payments are mostly capital and a smaller portion interest. In this way the payment amount determined at outset is calculated to ensure the loan is repaid at a specified date in the future. This gives borrowers assurance that by maintaining repayment the loan will be cleared at a specified date, if the interest rate does not change. Some lenders and 3rd parties offer a Bi-weekly mortgage payment program designed to accelerate the payoff of the loan.

Interest only

The main alternative to a capital and interest mortgage is an interest-only mortgage, where the capital is not repaid throughout the term. This type of mortgage is common in the UK, especially when associated with a regular investment plan. With this arrangement regular contributions are made to a separate investment plan designed to build up a lump sum to repay the mortgage at maturity. This type of arrangement is called an *investment-backed mortgage* or is often related to the type of plan used: endowment mortgage if an endowment policy is used, similarly a Personal Equity Plan (PEP) mortgage, Individual Savings Account (ISA) mortgage or pension mortgage. Historically, investment-backed mortgages offered various tax advantages over repayment mortgages, although this is no longer the case in the UK. Investment-backed mortgages are seen as higher risk as they are dependent on the investment making sufficient return to clear the debt.

Until recently it was not uncommon for interest only mortgages to be arranged without a repayment vehicle, with the borrower gambling that the property market will rise sufficiently for the loan to be repaid by trading down at retirement (or when rent on the property and inflation combine to surpass the interest rate).

No capital or interest

For older borrowers (typically in retirement), it may be possible to arrange a mortgage where neither the capital nor interest is repaid. The interest is rolled up with the capital, increasing the debt each year.

These arrangements are variously called reverse mortgages, lifetime mortgages or *equity release mortgages* (referring to home equity), depending on the country. The loans are typically not repaid until the borrowers die, hence the age restriction. For further details, see *equity release*.

Interest and partial capital

In the U.S. a partial amortization or balloon loan is one where the amount of monthly payments due are calculated (amortized) over a certain term, but the outstanding capital balance is due at some point short of that term. In the UK, a part repayment mortgage is quite common, especially where the original mortgage was investment-backed and on moving house further borrowing is arranged on a capital and interest (repayment) basis.

Variations

Graduated payment mortgage loan have increasing costs over time and are geared to young borrowers who expect wage increases over time. Balloon payment mortgages have only partial amortization, meaning that amount of monthly payments due are calculated (amortized) over a certain term, but the outstanding principal balance is due at some point short of that term, and at the end of the term a balloon payment is due. When interest rates are high relative to the rate on an existing seller's loan, the buyer can consider assuming the seller's mortgage.[7] A wraparound mortgage is a form of seller financing that can make it easier for a seller to sell a property. A biweekly mortgage has payments made every two weeks instead of monthly.

Budget loans include taxes and insurance in the mortgage payment;[8] package loans add the costs of furnishings and other personal property to the mortgage. Buydown mortgages allow the seller or lender to pay something similar to mortgage points to reduce interest rate and encourage buyers.[9] Homeowners can also take out equity loans in which they receive cash for a mortgage debt on their house. Shared appreciation mortgages are a form of equity release. In the US, foreign nationals due to their unique situation face Foreign National mortgage conditions.

Flexible mortgages allow for more freedom by the borrower to skip payments or prepay. Offset mortgages allow deposits to be counted against the mortgage loan. in the UK there is also the endowment mortgage where the borrowers pay interest while the principal is paid with a life insurance policy.

Commercial mortgages typically have different interest rates, risks, and contracts than personal loans. Participation mortgages allow multiple investors to share in a loan. Builders may take out blanket loans which cover several properties at once. Bridge loans may be used as temporary financing pending a longer-term loan. Hard money loans provide financing in exchange for the mortgaging of real estate collateral.

Foreclosure and non-recourse lending

In most jurisdictions, a lender may foreclose the mortgaged property if certain conditions - principally, non-payment of the mortgage loan - occur. Subject to local legal requirements, the property may then be sold. Any amounts received from the sale (net of costs) are applied to the original debt. In some jurisdictions, mortgage loans are non-recourse loans: if the funds recouped from sale of the mortgaged property are insufficient to cover the outstanding debt, the lender may not have recourse to the borrower after foreclosure. In other jurisdictions, the borrower remains responsible for any remaining debt.

In virtually all jurisdictions, specific procedures for foreclosure and sale of the mortgaged property apply, and may be tightly regulated by the relevant government. There are strict or judicial foreclosures and non-judicial foreclosures, also known as power of sale foreclosures. In some jurisdictions, foreclosure and sale can occur quite rapidly, while in others, foreclosure may take many months or even years. In many countries, the ability of lenders to foreclose is extremely limited, and mortgage market development has been notably slower.

Mortgage lending in Continental Europe

Within the European Union, the Covered bonds market volume (covered bonds outstanding) amounted to about EUR 2 trillion at year-end 2007 with Germany, Denmark, Spain, and France each having outstandings above 200,000 EUR million.[10] In German language, Pfandbriefe is the term applied. Pfandbrief-like securities have been introduced in more than 25 European countries – and in recent years also in the U.S. and other countries outside Europe – each with their own unique law and regulations. However, the diffusion of the concept differ: In 2000, the US institutions Fannie Mae and Freddie Mac together reached one per cent of the national population. Furthermore, 87 per cent of their purchased mortgages were granted to borrowers in metropolitan areas with higher income levels. In Europe, a wider market has been achieved: In Denmark, mortgage banks reached 35 per cent of the population in 2002, while the German Bausparkassen achieved widespread regional distribution and more than 30 per cent of the German population concluded a Bauspar contract (as of 2001).[11]

Costs

A study issued by the UN Economic Commission for Europe compared German, US, and Danish mortgage systems. The German Bausparkassen have reported nominal interest rates of approximately 6 per cent per annum in the last 40 years (as of 2004). In addition, they charge administration and service fees (about 1.5 per cent of the loan amount). In the United States, the average interest rates for fixed-rate mortgages in the housing market started in the tens and twenties in the 1980s and have (as of 2004) reached about 6 per cent per annum. However, gross borrowing costs are substantially higher than the nominal interest rate and amounted for the last 30 years to 10.46 per cent. In Denmark, similar to the United States capital market, interest rates have fallen to 6 per cent per annum. A risk and administration fee amounts to 0.5 per cent of the outstanding debt. In addition, an acquisition fee is charged which amounts to one per cent of the principal.[11]

Recent trends

On July 28, 2008, US Treasury Secretary Henry Paulson announced that, along with four large U.S. banks, the Treasury would attempt to kick start a market for these securities in the United States, primarily to provide an alternative form of mortgage-backed securities.[12] Similarly, in the UK "the Government is inviting views on options for a UK framework to deliver more affordable long-term fixed-rate mortgages, including the lessons to be learned from international markets and institutions".[13]

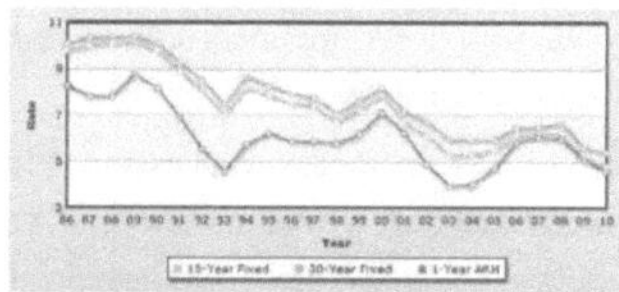
Mortgage Rates Historical Trends 1986 to 2010

George Soros's October 10, 2008 Wall Street Journal editorial promoted the Danish mortgage market model.[14] A survey of European Pfandbrief-like products was issued in 2005 by the Bank for International Settlements;[15] the International Monetary Fund in 2007 issued a study of the covered bond markets in Germany and Spain,[16] while the European Central Bank in 2003 issued a study of housing markets, addressing also mortgage markets and providing a two page overview of current mortgage systems in the EU countries.[17]

History

While the idea originated in Prussia in 1769, a Danish act on mortgage credit associations of 1850 enabled the issuing of bonds (Danish: Realkreditobligationer) as a means to refinance mortgage loans. With the German mortgage banks law of 1900, the whole German Empire was given a standardized legal foundation for the emission of Pfandbriefe. An account from the perspective of development economics is available.[18]

Mortgage insurance

Mortgage insurance is an insurance policy designed to protect the mortgagee (lender) from any default by the mortgagor (borrower). It is used commonly in loans with a loan-to-value ratio over 80%, and employed in the event of foreclosure and repossession.

This policy is typically paid for by the borrower as a component to final nominal (note) rate, or in one lump sum up front, or as a separate and itemized component of monthly mortgage payment. In the last case, mortgage insurance can be dropped when the lender informs the borrower, or its subsequent assigns, that the property has appreciated, the loan has been paid down, or any combination of both to relegate the loan-to-value under 80%.

In the event of repossession, banks, investors, etc. must resort to selling the property to recoup their original investment (the money lent), and are able to dispose of hard assets (such as real estate) more quickly by reductions in price. Therefore, the mortgage insurance acts as a hedge should the repossessing authority recover less than full and fair market value for any hard asset.

Islamic mortgages

Islamic Sharia law prohibits the payment or receipt of interest, meaning that Muslims cannot use conventional mortgages. However, real estate is far too expensive for most people to buy outright using cash: Islamic mortgages solve this problem by having the property change hands twice. In one variation, the bank will buy the house outright and then act as a landlord. The homebuyer, in addition to paying rent, will pay a contribution towards the purchase of the property. When the last payment is made, the property changes hands.

Typically, this may lead to a higher final price for the buyers. This is because in some countries (such as the United Kingdom and India) there is a Stamp Duty which is a tax charged by the government on a change of ownership. Because ownership changes twice in an Islamic mortgage, a stamp tax may be charged twice. Many other jurisdictions have similar transaction taxes on change of ownership which may be levied. In the United Kingdom, the dual application of Stamp Duty in such transactions was removed in the Finance Act 2003 in order to facilitate Islamic mortgages.[19]

An alternative scheme involves the bank reselling the property according to an installment plan, at a price higher than the original price.

Both of these methods compensate the lender as if they were charging interest, but the loans are structured in a way that in name they are not, and the lender shares the financial risks involved in the transaction with the homebuyer.

See also

General, or related to more than one nation

- Commercial mortgage
- Nonrecourse debt
- Refinancing
- No Income No Asset (NINA)
- Annual percentage rate

Related to the United Kingdom

- Buy to let
- Remortgage
- UK mortgage terminology

Related to the United States

- Commercial lender (US) - a term for a lender collateralizing non-residential properties.
- Fixed rate mortgage calculations (USA)
- pre-qualification - U.S. mortgage terminology
- pre-approval - U.S. mortgage terminology
- FHA loan - Relating to the U.S. Federal Housing Administration
- VA loan - Relating to the U.S. Veterans Administration.
- eMortgages
- Location Efficient Mortgage - a type of mortgage for urban areas
- Predatory mortgage lending

Other nations

- Danish mortgage market
- Mortgage Investment Corporation

Legal details

- Deed - legal aspects
- Mechanics lien - a legal concept
- Perfection - applicable legal filing requirements

References

[1] Sonia Kolesnikov-Jessop (January 29, 2009). "Bali's cash property market keeps prices up" (http://www.iht.com/articles/2009/01/29/properties/rebali.1-395765.php). International Herald-Tribune. . Retrieved 2009-01-30. "'In Bali, there are no mortgages available, so everyone who owns a house here has paid cash for it,' said Nils Wetterlind, managing director of Tropical Homes, a real estate developer and brokerage based on the island."

[2] Coke, Edward. *Commentaries on the Laws of England*. "[I]f he doth not pay, then the Land which is put in pledge upon condition for the payment of the money, is taken from him for ever, and so dead to him upon condition, &c. And if he doth pay the money, then the pledge is dead as to the Tenant"

[3] "Personal finance glossary" (http://www.mortgageloan.com/finance-glossary/mortgage_loan). . Retrieved 18 January 2011.

[4] FTC. Mortgage Servicing: Making Sure Your Payments Count (http://www.ftc.gov/bcp/edu/pubs/consumer/homes/rea10.shtm).

[5] "Who Needs Mortgage Loan Insurance?" (http://www.cmhc-schl.gc.ca/en/co/moloin/moloin_002.cfm). Canadian Mortgage and Housing Corporation. . Retrieved 2009-01-30.

[6] "Some info on Homeowner Loans" (http://www.loansforpeoplewithbadcredit.biz/badcreditblog/general-articles/some-info-on-homeowner-loans/). Loans for people with bad credit. 1 October 2011. . Retrieved 14 October 2011.

[7] Are Mortgage Assumptions a Good Deal? (http://www.mtgprofessor.com/A - Options/are_assumptions_a_good_deal.htm). Mortgage Professor.

[8] Cortesi GR. (2003). *Mastering Real Estate Principles*. p. 371

[9] Homes: Slow-market savings - the 'buy-down' (http://money.cnn.com/2006/11/13/real_estate/the_buy_down/index.htm?postversion=2006111316). *CNN Money*.

[10] Covered Bond Outstanding 2007 (http://ecbc.hypo.org/content/Default.asp?PageID=320)

[11] Housing Finance Systems for countries in Transition - Principles and Examples. United Nations, New York and Geneva, 2005, p. 45 (http://www.unece.org/hlm/prgm/hmm/hsg_finance/publications/housing.finance.system.pdf)

[12] FDIC Policy Statement on Covered Bonds (http://www.fdic.gov/news/news/press/2008/pr08060a.html)

[13] Housing Finance Review: analysis and proposals. HM Treasury, March 2008 (http://www.hm-treasury.gov.uk/media/6/4/bud08_housing_787_.pdf)

[14] "Denmark offers a model mortgage market" (http://online.wsj.com/article/SB122360660328622015.html)

[15] Mastroeni, O (2005) Pfandbrief-style products in Europe (http://www.bis.org/publ/bppdf/bispap05b.pdf). Bank for International Settlements (BIS) (http://www.bis.org/): BIS Papers No 5, 22 Jan 2008

[16] The Use of Mortgage Covered Bonds, Renzo G. Avesani, Antonio García Pascual,and Elina Ribakova. 2007 International Monetary Fund, IMF Working Paper, WP/07/20, January 2007. 23 p. (http://www.imf.org/external/pubs/ft/wp/2007/wp0720.pdf)

[17] European Central Bank (http://www.ecb.int): Structural factors in the EU housing markets, March 2003 (http://www.ecb.int/pub/pdf/other/euhousingmarketsen.pdf)

[18] Guinnane TW, Ghatak M (1999) The Economics of Lending with Joint Liability: Theory and Practice. *Journal of Development Economics*, Vol 60, 195-228, jfr. University of Copenhagen, Department of Economics, Discussion Papers, No 98-16: The Economics of Lending with Joint Liability: Theory and Practice, by Maitreesh Ghatak & Timothy W. Guinnane

[19] Reliefs: Alternative property finance (http://www.hmrc.gov.uk/manuals/sdltmanual/SDLTM28400.htm)

External links

- Mortgages (http://www.dmoz.org/Business/Financial_Services/Mortgages//) at the Open Directory Project
- FHA loans (http://www.hud.gov/buying/loans.cfm) (Department of Housing and Urban Development)
- Mortgages: For Home Buyers and Homeowners (http://www.usa.gov/shopping/realestate/mortgages/mortgages.shtml) at USA.gov
- Financial Consumer Agency of Canada

Credit card

A **credit card** is a small plastic card issued to users as a system of payment. It allows its holder to buy goods and services based on the holder's promise to pay for these goods and services.[1] The issuer of the card creates a revolving account and grants a line of credit to the consumer (or the user) from which the user can borrow money for payment to a merchant or as a cash advance to the user.

Credit card

A credit card is different from a charge card: a charge card requires the balance to be paid in full each month.[2] In contrast, credit cards allow the consumers a continuing balance of debt, subject to interest being charged. A credit card also differs from a cash card, which can be used like currency by the owner of the card. Most credit cards are issued by banks or credit unions, and are the shape and size specified by the ISO/IEC 7810 standard as ID-1. This is defined as 85.60 × 53.98 mm (3.370 × 2.125 in) ($3^3/_8$ × $2^1/_8$ in) in size.

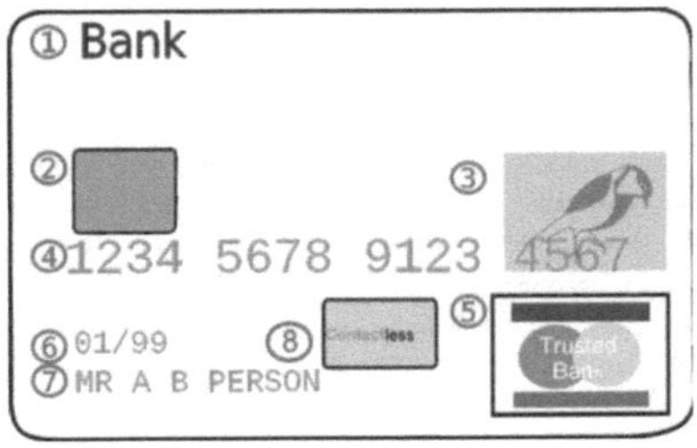

An example of the front in a typical credit card: Issuing bank logo EMVEMV chip on "smart cards" HologramCredit card numberCard brand logo Expiration Date Card Holder Name contactless chip

History

The concept of using a card for purchases was described in 1887 by Edward Bellamy in his utopian novel *Looking Backward*. Bellamy used the term *credit card* eleven times in this novel.[3]

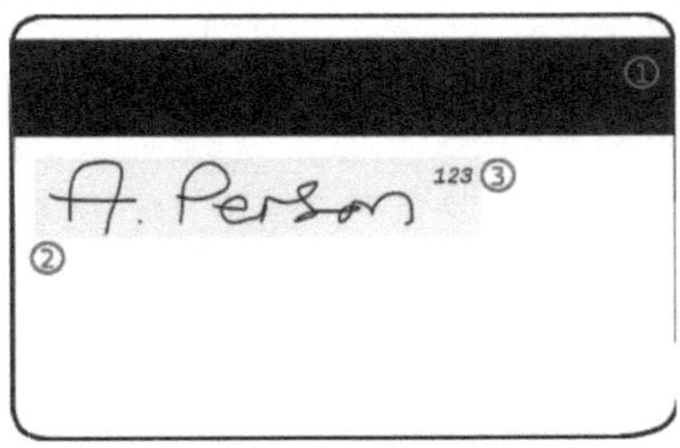

An example of the reverse side of a typical credit card: Magnetic stripe#Financial cardsMagnetic StripeSignature Strip Card Security Code

The modern credit card was the successor of a variety of merchant credit schemes. It was first used in the 1920s, in the United States, specifically to sell fuel to a growing number of automobile owners. In 1938 several companies started to accept each other's cards. Western Union had begun issuing charge cards to its frequent customers in 1921. Some charge cards were printed on paper card stock, but were easily counterfeited.

The Charga-Plate, developed in 1928, was an early predecessor to the credit card and used in the U.S. from the 1930s to the late 1950s. It was a 2½" × 1¼" rectangle of sheet metal related to Addressograph and military dog tag systems. It was embossed with the customer's name, city and state. It held a small paper card for a signature. In recording a purchase, the plate was laid into a recess in the imprinter, with a paper "charge slip" positioned on top of it. The record of the transaction included an impression of the embossed information, made by the imprinter pressing an inked ribbon against the charge slip.[4] Charga-Plate was a trademark of Farrington Manufacturing Co. Charga-Plates were issued by large-scale merchants to their regular customers, much like department store credit cards of today. In some cases, the plates were kept in the issuing store rather than held by customers. When an authorized user made a purchase, a clerk retrieved the plate from the store's files and then processed the purchase. Charga-Plates speeded back-office bookkeeping that was done manually in paper ledgers in each store, before computers.

In 1936, American Airlines and the Air Transport Association simplified the process even more with the advent of the Air Travel Card. They created a numbering scheme that identified the Issuer of card as well as the Customer account. This is the reason the modern UATP cards still start with the number 1. With an Air Travel Card passengers could "buy now, and pay later" for a ticket against their credit and receive a fifteen percent discount at any of the accepting airlines. By the 1940s, all of the major domestic airlines offered Air Travel Cards that could be used on 17 different airlines. By 1941 about half of the Airlines Revenues came through the Air Travel Card agreement. The Airlines had also started offering installment plans to lure new travelers into the air. In October 1948 the Air Travel Card become the first inter-nationally valid Charge Card within all members of the International Air Transport Association.

The concept of customers paying different merchants using the same card was expanded in 1950 by Ralph Schneider and Frank McNamara, founders of Diners Club, to consolidate multiple cards. The Diners Club, which was created partially through a merger with Dine and Sign, produced the first "general purpose" charge card, and required the entire bill to be paid with each statement. That was followed by Carte Blanche and in 1958 by American Express which created a worldwide credit card network (although these were initially charge cards that acquired credit card features after BankAmericard demonstrated the feasibility of the concept).

However, until 1958, no one had been able to create a working *revolving credit* financial instrument issued by a third-party bank that was generally accepted by a large number of merchants (as opposed to merchant-issued revolving cards accepted by only a few merchants). A dozen experiments by small American banks had been attempted (and had failed). In September 1958, Bank of America launched the *BankAmericard* in Fresno, California. BankAmericard became the first successful recognizably modern credit card (although it underwent a troubled gestation during which its creator resigned), and with its overseas affiliates, eventually evolved into the Visa system. In 1966, the ancestor of MasterCard was born when a group of California banks established Master Charge to compete with BankAmericard; it received a significant boost when Citibank merged its proprietary Everything Card (launched in 1967) into Master Charge in 1969.

Early credit cards in the U.S., of which BankAmericard was the most prominent example, were mass produced and mass mailed unsolicited to bank customers who were thought to be good credit risks. But, "They have been mailed off to unemployables, drunks, narcotics addicts and to compulsive debtors, a process President Johnson's Special Assistant Betty Furness found very like 'giving sugar to diabetics'."[5] These mass mailings were known as "drops" in banking terminology, and were outlawed in 1970 due to the financial chaos they caused, but not before 100 million credit cards had been dropped into the U.S. population. After 1970, only credit card applications could be sent unsolicited in mass mailings.

The fractured nature of the U.S. banking system under the Glass–Steagall Act meant that credit cards became an effective way for those who were traveling around the country to move their credit to places where they could not directly use their banking facilities. In 1966 Barclaycard in the UK launched the first credit card outside of the U.S.

There are now countless variations on the basic concept of revolving credit for individuals (as issued by banks and honored by a network of financial institutions), including organization-branded credit cards, corporate-user credit cards, store cards and so on.

Although credit cards reached very high adoption levels in the US, Canada and the UK in the mid twentieth century, many cultures were more cash-oriented, or developed alternative forms of cash-less payments, such as Carte bleue or the Eurocard (Germany, France, Switzerland, and others). In these places, adoption of credit cards was initially much slower. It took until the 1990s to reach anything like the percentage market-penetration levels achieved in the US, Canada, or UK. In some countries, acceptance still remains poor as the use of a credit card system depends on the banking system being perceived as reliable. Japan remains a very cash oriented society, with credit card adoption being limited to only the largest of merchants, although an alternative system based on RFIDs inside cellphones has seen some acceptance. Because of strict regulations regarding banking system overdrafts, some countries, France in particular, were much faster to develop and adopt chip-based credit cards which are now seen as major anti-fraud credit devices. Debit cards and online banking are used more widely than credit cards in some countries.

The design of the credit card itself has become a major selling point in recent years. The value of the card to the issuer is often related to the customer's usage of the card, or to the customer's financial worth. This has led to the rise of Co-Brand and Affinity cards - where the card design is related to the "affinity" (a university or professional society, for example) leading to higher card usage. In most cases a percentage of the value of the card is returned to the affinity group.

Collectible credit cards

A growing field of numismatics (study of money), or more specifically exonumia (study of money-like objects), credit card collectors seek to collect various embodiments of credit from the now familiar plastic cards to older paper merchant cards, and even metal tokens that were accepted as merchant credit cards. Early credit cards were made of celluloid plastic, then metal and fiber, then paper, and are now mostly plastic.

How credit cards work

Credit cards are issued by a credit card issuer, such as a bank or credit union, after an account has been approved by the credit provider, after which cardholders can use it to make purchases at merchants accepting that card. Merchants often advertise which cards they accept by displaying acceptance marks – generally derived from logos – or may communicate this orally, as in "Credit cards are fine" (implicitly meaning "major brands"), "We take (brands X, Y, and Z)", or "We don't take credit cards".

When a purchase is made, the credit card user agrees to pay the card issuer. The cardholder indicates consent to pay by signing a receipt with a record of the card details and indicating the amount to be paid or by entering a personal identification number (PIN). Also, many merchants now accept verbal authorizations via telephone and electronic authorization using the Internet, known as a card not present transaction (CNP).

Electronic verification systems allow merchants to verify in a few seconds that the card is valid and the credit card customer has sufficient credit to cover the purchase, allowing the verification to happen at time of purchase. The verification is performed using a credit card payment terminal or point-of-sale (POS) system with a communications link to the merchant's acquiring bank. Data from the card is obtained from a magnetic stripe or chip on the card; the latter system is called Chip and PIN in the United Kingdom and Ireland, and is implemented as an EMV card.

For card not present transactions where the card is not shown (e.g., e-commerce, mail order, and telephone sales), merchants additionally verify that the customer is in physical possession of the card and is the authorized user by asking for additional information such as the security code printed on the back of the card, date of expiry, and billing address.

Each month, the credit card user is sent a statement indicating the purchases undertaken with the card, any outstanding fees, and the total amount owed. After receiving the statement, the cardholder may dispute any charges that he or she thinks are incorrect (see 15 U.S.C. § 1643 [6], which limits cardholder liability for unauthorized use of a credit card to $50, and the Fair Credit Billing Act for details of the US regulations). Otherwise, the cardholder must pay a defined minimum proportion of the bill by a due date, or may choose to pay a higher amount up to the entire amount owed. The credit issuer charges interest on the amount owed if the balance is not paid in full (typically at a much higher rate than most other forms of debt). In addition, if the credit card user fails to make at least the minimum payment by the due date, the issuer may impose a "late fee" and/or other penalties on the user. To help mitigate this, some financial institutions can arrange for automatic payments to be deducted from the user's bank accounts, thus avoiding such penalties altogether as long as the cardholder has sufficient funds.

Advertising, solicitation, application and approval

Credit card advertising regulations include the Schumer box disclosure requirements. A large fraction of junk mail consists of credit card offers created from lists provided by the major credit reporting agencies. In the United States, the three major US credit bureaus (Equifax, TransUnion and Experian) allow consumers to opt out from related credit card solicitation offers via its Opt Out Pre Screen program.

Interest charges

Credit card issuers usually waive interest charges if the balance is paid in full each month, but typically will charge full interest on the entire outstanding balance from the date of each purchase if the total balance is not paid.

For example, if a user had a $1,000 transaction and repaid it in full within this grace period, there would be no interest charged. If, however, even $1.00 of the total amount remained unpaid, interest would be charged on the $1,000 from the date of purchase until the payment is received. The precise manner in which interest is charged is usually detailed in a cardholder agreement which may be summarized on the back of the monthly statement. The general calculation formula most financial institutions use to determine the amount of interest to be charged is APR/100 x ADB/365 x number of days revolved. Take the annual percentage rate (APR) and divide by 100 then multiply to the amount of the average daily balance (ADB) divided by 365 and then take this total and multiply by the total number of days the amount revolved before payment was made on the account. Financial institutions refer to interest charged back to the original time of the transaction and up to the time a payment was made, if not in full, as RRFC or residual retail finance charge. Thus after an amount has revolved and a payment has been made, the user of the card will still receive interest charges on their statement after paying the next statement in full (in fact the statement may only have a charge for interest that collected up until the date the full balance was paid, i.e. when the balance stopped revolving).

The credit card may simply serve as a form of revolving credit, or it may become a complicated financial instrument with multiple balance segments each at a different interest rate, possibly with a single umbrella credit limit, or with separate credit limits applicable to the various balance segments. Usually this compartmentalization is the result of special incentive offers from the issuing bank, to encourage balance transfers from cards of other issuers. In the event that several interest rates apply to various balance segments, payment allocation is generally at the discretion of the issuing bank, and payments will therefore usually be allocated towards the lowest rate balances until paid in full before any money is paid towards higher rate balances. Interest rates can vary considerably from card to card, and the interest rate on a particular card may jump dramatically if the card user is late with a payment on that card *or any other credit instrument*, or even if the issuing bank decides to raise its revenue.

Benefits to customers

The main benefit to each customer is convenience. Compared to debit cards and cheques, a credit card allows small short-term loans to be quickly made to a customer who need not calculate a balance remaining before every transaction, provided the total charges do not exceed the maximum credit line for the card. Credit cards also provide more fraud protection than debit cards. In the UK for example, the bank is jointly liable with the merchant for purchases of defective products over £100.[7]

Many credit cards offer rewards and benefits packages, such as offering enhanced product warranties at no cost, free loss/damage coverage on new purchases, and points which may be redeemed for cash, products, or airline tickets.

Detriments to customers

High interest and bankruptcy

Low introductory credit card rates are limited to a fixed term, usually between 6 and 12 months, after which a higher rate is charged. As all credit cards charge fees and interest, some customers become so indebted to their credit card provider that they are driven to bankruptcy. Some credit cards often levy a rate of 20 to 30 percent after a payment is missed; in other cases a fixed charge is levied without change to the interest rate. In some cases universal default may apply: the high default rate is applied to a card in good standing by missing a payment on an unrelated account from the same provider. This can lead to a snowball effect in which the consumer is drowned by unexpectedly high interest rates. Further, most card holder agreements enable the issuer to arbitrarily raise the interest rate for any reason they see fit. First Premier Bank at one point offered a credit card with a 79.9% interest rate,[8] however they pulled the plug on this card in February of 2011 because of persistant defaults.[9]

Complex fee structures in the credit card industry limit customers' ability to comparison shop, help ensure that the industry is not price-competitive and help maximize industry profits. [10]

Inflated pricing for all consumers

Merchants that accept credit cards must pay interchange fees and discount fees on all credit-card transactions.[11] [12] In some cases merchants are barred by their credit agreements from passing these fees directly to credit card customers, or from setting a minimum transaction amount (no longer prohibited in the United States).[13] The result is that merchants may charge all customers (including those who do not use credit cards) higher prices to cover the fees on credit card transactions.[12] In the United States in 2008 credit card companies collected a total of $48 billion in interchange fees, or an average of $427 per family, with an average fee rate of about 2% per transaction.[12]

Weakens self regulation

Several studies have shown that consumers are likely to spend more money when they pay by credit card. Researchers suggest that when people pay using credit cards, they do not experience the abstract pain of payment.[14] Furthermore, researchers have found that using credit cards can increase consumption of unhealthy food.[15]

Grace period

A credit card's grace period is the time the customer has to pay the balance before interest is assessed on the outstanding balance. Grace periods may vary, but usually range from 20 to 50 days depending on the type of credit card and the issuing bank. Some policies allow for reinstatement after certain conditions are met.

Usually, if a customer is late paying the balance, finance charges will be calculated and the grace period does not apply. Finance charges incurred depend on the grace period and balance; with most credit cards there is no grace period if there is any outstanding balance from the previous billing cycle or statement (i.e. interest is applied on both the previous balance and new transactions). However, there are some credit cards that will only apply finance charge on the previous or old balance, excluding new transactions.

Benefits to merchants

For merchants, a credit card transaction is often more secure than other forms of payment, such as cheques, because the issuing bank commits to pay the merchant the moment the transaction is authorized, regardless of whether the consumer defaults on the credit card payment (except for legitimate disputes, which are discussed below, and can result in charges back to the merchant). In most cases, cards are even more secure than cash, because they discourage theft by the merchant's employees and reduce the amount of cash on the premises.

An example of street markets accepting credit cards. Most simply display the acceptance marks (stylized logos, shown in the upper-left corner of the sign) of all the cards they accept.

Prior to credit cards, each merchant had to evaluate each customer's credit history before extending credit. That task is now performed by the banks which assume the credit risk. Credit cards can also aid in securing a sale, especially if the customer does not have enough cash on his or her person or checking account. Extra turnover is generated by the fact that the customer can purchase goods and/or services immediately and is less inhibited by the amount of cash in his or her pocket and the immediate state of his or her bank balance. Much of merchants' marketing is based on this immediacy.

For each purchase, the bank charges the merchant a commission (discount fee) for this service and there may be a certain delay before the agreed payment is received by the merchant. The commission is often a percentage of the transaction amount, plus a fixed fee (interchange rate). In addition, a merchant may be penalized or have their ability to receive payment using that credit card restricted if there are too many cancellations or reversals of charges as a result of disputes. Some small merchants require credit purchases to have a minimum amount to compensate for the transaction costs.

In some countries, for example the Nordic countries, banks guarantee payment on stolen cards only if an ID card is checked and the ID card number/civic registration number is written down on the receipt together with the signature. In these countries merchants therefore usually ask for ID. Non-Nordic citizens, who are unlikely to possess a Nordic ID card or driving license, will instead have to show their passport, and the passport number will be written down on the receipt, sometimes together with other information. Some shops use the card's PIN for identification, and in that case showing an ID card is not necessary.

Costs to merchants

Merchants are charged several fees for accepting credit cards. The merchant is usually charged a commission of around 1 to 3 percent of the value of each transaction paid for by credit card. The merchant may also pay a variable charge, called an interchange rate, for each transaction.[11] In some instances of very low-value transactions, use of credit cards will significantly reduce the profit margin or cause the merchant to lose money on the transaction. Merchants with very low average transaction prices or very high average transaction prices are more averse to accepting credit cards. In some cases merchants may charge users a "credit card supplement", either a fixed amount or a percentage, for payment by credit card.[16] This practice is prohibited by the credit card contracts in the United States, although the contracts allow the merchants to give discounts for cash payment.

Parties involved

- Cardholder: The holder of the card used to make a purchase; the consumer.
- Card-issuing bank: The financial institution or other organization that issued the credit card to the cardholder. This bank bills the consumer for repayment and bears the risk that the card is used fraudulently. American Express and Discover were previously the only card-issuing banks for their respective brands, but as of 2007, this is no longer the case. Cards issued by banks to cardholders in a different country are known as offshore credit cards.
- Merchant: The individual or business accepting credit card payments for products or services sold to the cardholder.
- Acquiring bank: The financial institution accepting payment for the products or services on behalf of the merchant.
- Independent sales organization: Resellers (to merchants) of the services of the acquiring bank.
- Merchant account: This could refer to the acquiring bank or the independent sales organization, but in general is the organization that the merchant deals with.
- Credit Card association: An association of card-issuing banks such as Discover, Visa, MasterCard, American Express, etc. that set transaction terms for merchants, card-issuing banks, and acquiring banks.
- Transaction network: The system that implements the mechanics of the electronic transactions. May be operated by an independent company, and one company may operate multiple networks.
- Affinity partner: Some institutions lend their names to an issuer to attract customers that have a strong relationship with that institution, and get paid a fee or a percentage of the balance for each card issued using their name. Examples of typical affinity partners are sports teams, universities, charities, professional organizations, and major retailers.

The flow of information and money between these parties — always through the card associations — is known as the interchange, and it consists of a few steps.

Transaction steps

- **Authorization**: The cardholder presents the card as payment to the merchant and the merchant submits the transaction to the acquirer (acquiring bank). The acquirer verifies the credit card number, the transaction type and the amount with the issuer (Card-issuing bank) and reserves that amount of the cardholder's credit limit for the merchant. An authorization will generate an approval code, which the merchant stores with the transaction.
- **Batching**: Authorized transactions are stored in "batches", which are sent to the acquirer. Batches are typically submitted once per day at the end of the business day. If a transaction is not submitted in the batch, the authorization will stay valid for a period determined by the issuer, after which the held amount will be returned to the cardholder's available credit (see authorization hold). Some transactions may be submitted in the batch without prior authorizations; these are either transactions falling under the merchant's floor limit or ones where the authorization was unsuccessful but the merchant still attempts to force the transaction through. (Such may be the case when the cardholder is not present but owes the merchant additional money, such as extending a hotel stay or car rental.)
- **Clearing and Settlement**: The acquirer sends the batch transactions through the credit card association, which debits the issuers for payment and credits the acquirer. Essentially, the issuer pays the acquirer for the transaction.
- **Funding**: Once the acquirer has been paid, the acquirer pays the merchant. The merchant receives the amount totaling the funds in the batch minus either the "discount rate," "mid-qualified rate", or "non-qualified rate" which are tiers of fees the merchant pays the acquirer for processing the transactions.
- **Chargebacks**: A chargeback is an event in which money in a merchant account is held due to a dispute relating to the transaction. Chargebacks are typically initiated by the cardholder. In the event of a chargeback, the issuer returns the transaction to the acquirer for resolution. The acquirer then forwards the chargeback to the merchant,

who must either accept the chargeback or contest it.

Secured credit cards

A secured credit card is a type of credit card secured by a deposit account owned by the cardholder. Typically, the cardholder must deposit between 100% and 200% of the total amount of credit desired. Thus if the cardholder puts down $1000, they will be given credit in the range of $500–$1000. In some cases, credit card issuers will offer incentives even on their secured card portfolios. In these cases, the deposit required may be significantly less than the required credit limit, and can be as low as 10% of the desired credit limit. This deposit is held in a special savings account. Credit card issuers offer this because they have noticed that delinquencies were notably reduced when the customer perceives something to lose if the balance is not repaid.

The cardholder of a secured credit card is still expected to make regular payments, as with a regular credit card, but should they default on a payment, the card issuer has the option of recovering the cost of the purchases paid to the merchants out of the deposit. The advantage of the secured card for an individual with negative or no credit history is that most companies report regularly to the major credit bureaus. This allows for building of positive credit history.

Although the deposit is in the hands of the credit card issuer as security in the event of default by the consumer, the deposit will not be debited simply for missing one or two payments. Usually the deposit is only used as an offset when the account is closed, either at the request of the customer or due to severe delinquency (150 to 180 days). This means that an account which is less than 150 days delinquent will continue to accrue interest and fees, and could result in a balance which is much higher than the actual credit limit on the card. In these cases the total debt may far exceed the original deposit and the cardholder not only forfeits their deposit but is left with an additional debt.

Most of these conditions are usually described in a cardholder agreement which the cardholder signs when their account is opened.

Secured credit cards are an option to allow a person with a poor credit history or no credit history to have a credit card which might not otherwise be available. They are often offered as a means of rebuilding one's credit. Fees and service charges for secured credit cards often exceed those charged for ordinary non-secured credit cards, however, for people in certain situations, (for example, after charging off on other credit cards, or people with a long history of delinquency on various forms of debt), secured cards are almost always more expensive then unsecured credit cards.

Sometimes a credit card will be secured by the equity in the borrower's home.

Prepaid "credit" cards

A **prepaid credit card** is not a true credit card,[17] since no credit is offered by the card issuer: the card-holder spends money which has been "stored" via a prior deposit by the card-holder or someone else, such as a parent or employer. However, it carries a credit-card brand (such as Discover, Visa, MasterCard, American Express, or JCB etc.) and can be used in similar ways just as though it were a regular credit card.[17] Unlike debit cards, prepaid credit cards generally do not require a PIN. An exception are prepaid credit cards with an EMV chip. These cards do require a PIN if the payment is processed via Chip and PIN technology.

After purchasing the card, the cardholder loads the account with any amount of money, up to the predetermined card limit and then uses the card to make purchases the same way as a typical credit card. Prepaid cards can be issued to minors (above 13) since there is no credit line involved. The main advantage over secured credit cards (see above section) is that you are not required to come up with $500 or more to open an account.[18] With prepaid credit cards purchasers are not charged any interest but are often charged a purchasing fee plus monthly fees after an arbitrary time period. Many other fees also usually apply to a prepaid card.[17]

Prepaid credit cards are sometimes marketed to teenagers[17] for shopping online without having their parents complete the transaction.[19]

Because of the many fees that apply to obtaining and using credit-card-branded prepaid cards, the Financial Consumer Agency of Canada describes them as "an expensive way to spend your own money".[20] The agency publishes a booklet entitled *Pre-paid Cards*[21] which explains the advantages and disadvantages of this type of prepaid card.

Features

As well as convenient, accessible credit, credit cards offer consumers an easy way to track expenses, which is necessary for both monitoring personal expenditures and the tracking of work-related expenses for taxation and reimbursement purposes. Credit cards are accepted worldwide, and are available with a large variety of credit limits, repayment arrangement, and other perks (such as rewards schemes in which points earned by purchasing goods with the card can be redeemed for further goods and services or credit card cashback).

Some countries, such as the United States, the United Kingdom, and France, limit the amount for which a consumer can be held liable due to fraudulent transactions as a result of a consumer's credit card being lost or stolen.

Security problems and solutions

Credit card security relies on the physical security of the plastic card as well as the privacy of the credit card number. Therefore, whenever a person other than the card owner has access to the card or its number, security is potentially compromised. Once, merchants would often accept credit card numbers without additional verification for mail order purchases. It's now common practice to only ship to confirmed addresses as a security measure to minimise fraudulent purchases. Some merchants will accept a credit card number for in-store purchases, whereupon access to the number allows easy fraud, but many require the card itself to be present, and require a signature. A lost or stolen card can be cancelled, and if this is done quickly, will greatly limit the fraud that can take place in this way. European banks can require a cardholder's security PIN be entered for in-person purchases with the card.

The PCI DSS is the security standard issued by The PCI SSC (Payment Card Industry Security Standards Council). This data security standard is used by acquiring banks to impose cardholder data security measures upon their merchants.

The goal of the credit card companies is not to eliminate fraud, but to "reduce it to manageable levels".[22] This implies that high-cost low-return fraud prevention measures will not be used if their cost exceeds the potential gains from fraud reduction - as would be expected from organisations whose goal is profit maximisation.

A smart card, combining credit card and debit card properties. The 3 by 5 mm security chip embedded in the card is shown enlarged in the inset. The contact pads on the card enable electronic access to the chip.

Internet fraud may be by claiming a chargeback which is not justified ("friendly fraud"), or carried out by the use of credit card information which can be stolen in many ways, the simplest being copying information from retailers, either online or offline. Despite efforts to improve security for remote purchases using credit cards, security breaches are usually the result of poor practice by merchants. For example, a website that safely uses SSL to encrypt card data from a client may then email the data, unencrypted, from the webserver to the merchant; or the merchant may store unencrypted details in a way that allows them to be accessed over the Internet or by a rogue employee; unencrypted card details are always a security risk. Even encryption data may be cracked.

Controlled Payment Numbers which are used by various banks such as Citibank (Virtual Account Numbers), Discover (Secure Online Account Numbers, Bank of America (Shop Safe), 5 banks using eCarte Bleue and CMB's Virtualis in France, and Swedbank of Sweden's eKort product are another option for protecting against credit card fraud. These are generally one-time use numbers that front one's actual account (debit/credit) number, and are generated as one shops on-line. They can be valid for a relatively short time, for the actual amount of the purchase, or for a price limit set by the user. Their use can be limited to one merchant. If the number given to the merchant is compromised, it will be rejected if an attempt is made to use it again.

A similar system of controls can be used on physical cards. Technology provides the option for banks to support many other controls too that can be turned on and off and varied by the credit card owner in real time as circumstances change (i.e., they can change temporal, numerical, geographical and many other parameters on their primary and subsidiary cards). Apart from the obvious benefits of such controls: from a security perspective this means that a customer can have a Chip and PIN card secured for the real world, and limited for use in the home country. In this eventuality a thief stealing the details will be prevented from using these overseas in non chip and pin (EMV) countries. Similarly the real card can be restricted from use on-line so that stolen details will be declined if this tried. Then when card users shop online they can use virtual account numbers. In both circumstances an alert system can be built in notifying a user that a fraudulent attempt has been made which breaches their parameters, and can provide data on this in real time. This is the optimal method of security for credit cards, as it provides very high levels of security, control and awareness in the real and virtual world.

Additionally, there are security features present on the physical card itself in order to prevent counterfeiting. For example, most modern credit cards have a watermark that will fluoresce under ultraviolet light. A Visa card has a letter V superimposed over the regular Visa logo and a Mastercard has the letters MC across the front of the card. Older Visa cards have a bald eagle or dove across the front. In the aforementioned cases, the security features are only visible under ultraviolet light and are invisible in normal light.

The Federal Bureau of Investigation and U.S. Postal Inspection Service are responsible for prosecuting criminals who engage in credit card fraud in the United States, but they do not have the resources to pursue all criminals. In general, federal officials only prosecute cases exceeding US$5,000. Three improvements to card security have been introduced to the more common credit card networks but none has proven to help reduce credit card fraud so far. First, the on-line verification system used by merchants is being enhanced to require a 4 digit Personal Identification Number (PIN) known only to the card holder. Second, the cards themselves are being replaced with similar-looking tamper-resistant smart cards which are intended to make forgery more difficult. The majority of smart card (IC card) based credit cards comply with the EMV (Europay MasterCard Visa) standard. Third, an additional 3 or 4 digit Card Security Code (CSC) is now present on the back of most cards, for use in card not present transactions. Stakeholders at all levels in electronic payment have recognized the need to develop consistent global standards for security that account for and integrate both current and emerging security technologies. They have begun to address these needs through organizations such as PCI DSS and the Secure POS Vendor Alliance.[23]

Code 10

Code 10 calls are made when merchants are suspicious about accepting a credit card.

The operator then asks the merchant a series of YES or NO questions to find out whether the merchant is suspicious of the card or the cardholder. The merchant may be asked to retain the card if it is safe to do so.

Credit history

The way credit card owners pay off their balances has a tremendous effect on their credit history. Two of the most important factors reported to a credit bureau are the timeliness of the debt payments and the amount of debt to credit limit. Lenders want to see payments made as agreed, usually on a monthly basis, and a credit balance of around one-third the credit limit. The credit information stays on the credit report generally for 7 years. However, there are a few jurisdictions and situations where the timeframe might differ.

Profits and losses

In recent times, credit card portfolios have been very profitable for banks, largely due to the booming economy of the late nineties. However, in the case of credit cards, such high returns go hand in hand with risk, since the business is essentially one of making unsecured (uncollateralized) loans, and thus dependent on borrowers not to default in large numbers.

Costs

Credit card issuers (banks) have several types of costs:

Interest expenses

Banks generally borrow the money they then lend to their customers. As they receive very low-interest loans from other firms, they may borrow as much as their customers require, while lending their capital to other borrowers at higher rates. If the card issuer charges 15% on money lent to users, and it costs 5% to borrow the money to lend, and the balance sits with the cardholder for a year, the issuer earns 10% on the loan. This 10% difference is the "net interest spread" and the 5% is the "interest expense".

Operating costs

This is the cost of running the credit card portfolio, including everything from paying the executives who run the company to printing the plastics, to mailing the statements, to running the computers that keep track of every cardholder's balance, to taking the many phone calls which cardholders place to their issuer, to protecting the customers from fraud rings. Depending on the issuer, marketing programs are also a significant portion of expenses.

Charge offs

When a consumer becomes severely delinquent on a debt (often at the point of six months without payment), the creditor may declare the debt to be a charge-off. It will then be listed as such on the debtor's credit bureau reports (Equifax, for instance, lists "R9" in the "status" column to denote a charge-off.)

A charge-off is considered to be "written off as uncollectable." To banks, bad debts and even fraud are simply part of the cost of doing business.

However, the debt is still legally valid, and the creditor can attempt to collect the full amount for the time periods permitted under state law, which is usually 3 to 7 years. This includes contacts from internal collections staff, or more likely, an outside collection agency. If the amount is large (generally over \$1500–\$2000), there is the possibility of a lawsuit or arbitration.

Rewards

Many credit card customers receive rewards, such as frequent flyer points, gift certificates, or cash back as an incentive to use the card. Rewards are generally tied to purchasing an item or service on the card, which may or may not include balance transfers, cash advances, or other special uses. Depending on the type of card, rewards will generally cost the issuer between 0.25% and 2.0% of the spread. Networks such as Visa or MasterCard have increased their fees to allow issuers to fund their rewards system. Some issuers discourage redemption by forcing the cardholder to call customer service for rewards. On their servicing website, redeeming awards is usually a feature that is very well hidden by the issuers. With a fractured and competitive environment, rewards points cut dramatically into an issuer's bottom line, and rewards points and related incentives must be carefully managed to ensure a profitable portfolio. Unlike unused gift cards, in whose case the breakage in certain US states goes to the state's treasury, unredeemed credit card points are retained by the issuer.

Fraud

In relative numbers the values lost in bank card fraud are minor, calculated in 2006 at 7 cents per 100 dollars worth of transactions (7 basis points).[24] In 2004, in the UK, the cost of fraud was over £500 million.[25] When a card is stolen, or an unauthorized duplicate made, most card issuers will refund some or all of the charges that the customer has received for things they did not buy. These refunds will, in some cases, be at the expense of the merchant, especially in mail order cases where the merchant cannot claim sight of the card. In several countries, merchants will lose the money if no ID card was asked for, therefore merchants usually require ID card in these countries. Credit card companies generally guarantee the merchant will be paid on legitimate transactions regardless of whether the consumer pays their credit card bill. Most banking services have their own credit card services that handle fraud cases and monitor for any possible attempt at fraud. Employees that are specialized in doing fraud monitoring and investigation are often placed in Risk Management, Fraud and Authorization, or Cards and Unsecured Business. Fraud monitoring emphasizes minimizing fraud losses while making an attempt to track down those responsible and contain the situation. Credit card fraud is a major white collar crime that has been around for many decades, even with the advent of the chip based card (EMV) that was put into practice in some countries to prevent cases such as these. Even with the implementation of such measures, credit card fraud continues to be a problem.

Promotion

Promotional purchase is any purchase on which separate terms and conditions are set on each individual transaction unlike a standard purchase where the terms are set on the cardholder's account record and their pricing strategy. All promotional purchases that post to a particular account will be carrying its own balance called as Promotional Balance.

Revenues

Offsetting the costs are the following revenues:

Interchange fee

In addition to fees paid by the card holder, merchants must also pay interchange fees to the card-issuing bank and the card association.[26] [27] For a typical credit card issuer, interchange fee revenues may represent about a quarter of total revenues.[28]

These fees are typically from 1 to 6 percent of each sale, but will vary not only from merchant to merchant (large merchants can negotiate lower rates[28]), but also from card to card, with business cards and rewards cards generally costing the merchants more to process. The interchange fee that applies to a particular transaction is also affected by many other variables including: the type of merchant, the merchant's total card sales volume, the merchant's average transaction amount, whether the cards were physically present, how the information required for the transaction was received, the specific type of card, when the transaction was settled, and the authorized and settled transaction amounts. In some cases, merchants add a surcharge to the credit cards to cover the interchange fee, encouraging their customers to instead use cash, debit cards, or even cheques.

Interest on outstanding balances

Interest charges vary widely from card issuer to card issuer. Often, there are "teaser" rates in effect for initial periods of time (as low as zero percent for, say, six months), whereas regular rates can be as high as 40 percent. In the U.S. there is no federal limit on the interest or late fees credit card issuers can charge; the interest rates are set by the states, with some states such as South Dakota, having no ceiling on interest rates and fees, inviting some banks to establish their credit card operations there. Other states, for example Delaware, have very weak usury laws. The teaser rate no longer applies if the customer doesn't pay their bills on time, and is replaced by a penalty interest rate (for example, 23.99%) that applies retroactively.

Fees charged to customers

The major fees are for:

- Late payments or overdue payments
- Charges that result in exceeding the credit limit on the card (whether done deliberately or by mistake), called overlimit fees
- Returned cheque fees or payment processing fees (e.g. phone payment fee)
- Cash advances and convenience cheques (often 3% of the amount)
- Transactions in a foreign currency (as much as 3% of the amount). A few financial institutions do not charge a fee for this.
- Membership fees (annual or monthly), sometimes a percentage of the credit limit.
- Exchange rate loading fees (sometimes these might not be reported on the customer's statement, even when applied).[29] The variation of exchange rates applied by different credit cards can be very substantial, as much as 10% according to a Lonely Planet report in 2009.[30]

Over limit charges

Consumers who keep their account in good order by always staying within their credit limit, and always making at least the minimum monthly payment will see interest as the biggest expense from their card provider. Those who are not so careful and regularly surpass their credit limit or are late in making payments are exposed to multiple charges that were typically as high as £25 - £35 [31] until a ruling from the Office of Fair Trading[32] that they would presume charges over £12 to be unfair which led the majority of card providers to reduce their fees to exactly that level.

US

The Credit CARD Protection Act of 2009, that was signed into law by President Obama, requires that consumers "opt-in" to over-limit charges. Some card issuers have therefore commenced solicitations requesting customers to opt in to overlimit fees, presenting this as a benefit as it may avoid the possibility of a future transaction being declined. Other issuers have simply discontinued the practice of charging overlimit fees. Whether a customer opts in to the overlimit fee or not, banks will in practice have discretion as to whether they choose to authorize transactions above the credit limit or not. Of course, any approved over limit transactions will only result in an overlimit fee for those customers who have opted in to the fee. This legislation took effect on February 22, 2010.

UK

The higher level of fees originally charged were claimed to be designed to recoup the costs of the card operator's overall business and to ensure that the credit card business as a whole generated a profit, rather than simply recovering the cost to the provider of the limit breach which has been estimated as typically between £3-£4. Profiting from a customer's mistakes is arguably not permitted under UK common law, if the charges constitute penalties for breach of contract, or under the Unfair Terms In Consumer Regulations 1999.

Subsequent rulings in respect of personal current accounts suggest that the argument that these charges are penalties for breach of contract is weak, and given the OFT's ruling it seems unlikely that any further test case will take place.

Whilst the law remains in the balance, many consumers have made claims against their credit cards providers for the charges that they have incurred, plus interest that they would have earned had the money not been deducted from their account. It is likely that claims for amounts charged in excess of £12 will succeed, but claims for charges at the OFT's £12 threshold level are more contentious.

Neutral consumer resources

Canada

The Government of Canada maintains a database of the fees, features, interest rates and reward programs of nearly 200 credit cards available in Canada. This database is updated on a quarterly basis with information supplied by the credit card issuing companies. Information in the database is published every quarter on the website of the Financial Consumer Agency of Canada (FCAC).

Information in the database is published in two formats. It is available in PDF comparison tables that break down the information according to type of credit card, allowing the reader to compare the features of, for example, all the student credit cards in the database.

The database also feeds into an interactive tool on the FCAC website.[33] The interactive tool uses several interview-type questions to build a profile of the user's credit card usage habits and needs, eliminating unsuitable choices based on the profile, so that the user is presented with a small number of credit cards and the ability to carry out detailed comparisons of features, reward programs, interest rates, etc.

Controversy

Credit card debt has increased steadily. Since the late 1990s, lawmakers, consumer advocacy groups, college officials and other higher education affiliates have become increasingly concerned about the rising use of credit cards among college students. The major credit card companies have been accused of targeting a younger audience, in particular college students, many of whom are already in debt with college tuition fees and college loans and who typically are less experienced at managing their own finances. Credit card debt may also negatively affect their grades as they are likely to work more both part and full time positions.[34]

Another controversial area is the universal default feature of many North American credit card contracts. When a cardholder is late paying a particular credit card issuer, that card's interest rate can be raised, often considerably. With universal default, a customer's *other* credit cards, for which the customer may be current on payments, may *also* have their rates and/or credit limit changed. The universal default feature allows creditors to periodically check cardholders' credit portfolios to view trade, allowing these other institutions to decrease the credit limit and/or increase rates on cardholders who may be late with another credit card issuer. Being late on one credit card will potentially affect all the cardholder's credit cards. Citibank voluntarily stopped this practice in March 2007 and Chase stopped the practice in November 2007.[35] The fact that credit card companies can change the interest rate on debts that were incurred when a different rate of interest was in place is similar to adjustable rate mortgages where interest rates on current debt may rise. However, in both cases this is agreed to in advance, and is a trade off that allows a lower initial rate as well as the possibility of an even lower rate (mortgages, if interest rates fall) or perpetually keeping a below-market rate (credit cards, if the user makes their debt payments on time). It should be noted that the Universal Default practice was actually *encouraged* by Federal Regulators, particularly those at the Office of the Comptroller of the Currency (OCC) as a means of managing the changing risk profiles of cardholders.

Another controversial area is the trailing interest issue. Trailing interest is the practice of charging interest on the entire bill no matter what percentage of it is paid. U.S Senator Carl Levin raised the issue of millions of Americans affected by hidden fees, compounding interest and cryptic terms. Their woes were heard in a Senate Permanent Subcommittee on Investigations hearing which was chaired by Senator Levin, who said that he intends to keep the spotlight on credit card companies and that legislative action may be necessary to purge the industry.[36] In 2009, the C.A.R.D. Act was signed into law, enacting protections for many of the issues Levin had raised.

In the United States, some have called for Congress to enact additional regulations on the industry; to expand the disclosure box clearly disclosing rate hikes, use plain language, incorporate balance payoff disclosures, and also to outlaw universal default. At a congress hearing around March 1, 2007, Citibank announced it would no longer practice this, effective immediately. Opponents of such regulation argue that customers must become more proactive and self-responsible in evaluating and negotiating terms with credit providers. Some of the nation's influential top credit card issuers, who are among the top fifty corporate contributors to political campaigns, successfully opposed it.

Hidden costs

In the United Kingdom, merchants won the right through The Credit Cards (Price Discrimination) Order 1990[37] to charge customers different prices according to the payment method. As of 2007, the United Kingdom was one of the world's most credit-card-intensive countries, with 2.4 credit cards per consumer, according to the UK Payments Administration Ltd.[38]

In the United States until 1984, federal law prohibited surcharges on card transactions. Although the federal Truth in Lending Act provisions that prohibited surcharges expired that year, a number of states have since enacted laws that continue to outlaw the practice; California, Colorado, Connecticut, Florida, Kansas, Massachusetts, Maine, New York, Oklahoma, and Texas have laws against surcharges. As of 2006, the United States probably had one of the world's highest if not the top ratio of credit cards per capita, with 984 million bank-issued Visa and MasterCard credit card and debit card accounts alone for an adult population of roughly 220 million people.[39] The credit card per US capita ratio was nearly 4:1 as of 2003[40] and as high as 5:1 as of 2006.[41]

Credit card numbering

The numbers found on credit cards have a certain amount of internal structure, and share a common numbering scheme.

The card number's *prefix*, called the Bank Identification Number, is the sequence of digits at the beginning of the number that determine the bank to which a credit card number belongs. This is the first six digits for MasterCard and Visa cards. The next nine digits are the individual account number, and the final digit is a validity check code.

In addition to the main credit card number, credit cards also carry issue and expiration dates (given to the nearest month), as well as extra codes such as issue numbers and security codes. Not all credit cards have the same sets of extra codes nor do they use the same number of digits.

Credit cards in ATMs

Many credit cards can also be used in an ATM to withdraw money against the credit limit extended to the card, but many card issuers charge interest on cash advances before they do so on purchases. The interest on cash advances is commonly charged from the date the withdrawal is made, rather than the monthly billing date. Many card issuers levy a commission for cash withdrawals, even if the ATM belongs to the same bank as the card issuer. Merchants do not offer cashback on credit card transactions because they would pay a percentage commission of the additional cash amount to their bank or merchant services provider, thereby making it uneconomical.

Many credit card companies will also, when applying payments to a card, do so at the end of a billing cycle, and apply those payments to everything before cash advances. For this reason, many consumers have large cash balances, which have no grace period and incur interest at a rate that is (usually) higher than the purchase rate, and will carry those balance for years, even if they pay off their statement balance each month.

Credit cards as funding for entrepreneurs

Credit cards are a risky way for entrepreneurs to acquire capital for their start ups when more conventional financing is unavailable. It's widely reported that Len Bosack and Sandy Lerner used personal credit cards[42] to start Cisco Systems. It is rumoured that Larry Page and Sergey Brin's start up of Google was financed by credit cards to buy the necessary computers and office equipment, more specifically "a terabyte of hard disks".[43] Similarly, filmmaker Robert Townsend financed part of *Hollywood Shuffle* using credit cards.[44] Director Kevin Smith funded *Clerks* in part by maxing out several credit cards. Actor Richard Hatch also financed his production of *Battlestar Galactica: The Second Coming* partly through his credit cards. Famed hedge fund manager Bruce Kovner began his career (and, later on, his firm Caxton Associates) in financial markets by borrowing from his credit card. UK entrepreneur James Caan (as seen on Dragon's Den) financed his first business using several credit cards.

See also

- Accountable Fundraising
- Bank card number
- Credit card associations
  - American Express
  - Diners Club
  - Discover Card
  - Entrust Bankcard
  - Japan Credit Bureau
  - MasterCard
  - Visa
- Credit card fraud
- Credit card hijacking
- Credit history
- Credit rating agency
- Credit reference agency
- Compulsive shopping
- Dynamic currency conversion, or DCC
- Electronic money
- Fair Credit Reporting Act
- Identity theft
- Interchange fee
- International Card Manufacturers Association
- Merchant account
- Point of sale
- Reimbursement
- Revolving account
- Stoozing
- Stored-value card

References

[1] Sullivan, arthur; Steven M. Sheffrin (2003). *Economics: Principles in action* (http://www.pearsonschool.com/index.cfm?locator=PSZ3R9&PMDbSiteId=2781&PMDbSolutionId=6724&PMDbCategoryId=&PMDbProgramId=12881&level=4). Upper Saddle River, New Jersey 07458: Pearson Prentice Hall. p. 261. ISBN 0-13-063085-3..

[2] Schneider, Gary (2010). *Electronic Commerce*. Cambridge: Course Technology. p. 497. ISBN 0538469242.

[3] (Chapters 9, 10, 11, 13, 25 and 26) and 3 times (Chapters 4, 8 and 19) in its sequel, *Equality*

[4] "Credit card imprinter" (http://cultureandcommunication.org/deadmedia/index.php/Credit_Card_Imprinter). Cultureandcommunication.org.. Retrieved 2011-07-28.

[5] Paul O'Neill, "A Little Gift from Your Friendly Banker", LIFE, April 27, 1970

[6] http://www.law.cornell.edu/uscode/15/1643.html

[7] "FAQ's" (http://www.theukcardsassociation.org.uk/misc/-/page/faqs/#question2). UK Cards Association. 2005-01-01.. Retrieved 2011-07-28.

[8] Prater, Connie (2010-04-07). "Issuer of 79.9% interest rate credit card defends its product" (http://www.foxbusiness.com/personal-finance/2009/12/18/issuer-rate-credit-card-defends-product/). FoxBusiness.com.. Retrieved 2011-07-28.

[9] Didier, Paul (2011-03-04). "The worst credit card in America is dead!" (http://www.debt800.com/news/news34.html). Debt800.com.. Retrieved 2011-08-23.

[10] Michael Simkovic, "The Effect of BAPCPA on Credit Card Industry Profits and Prices" (http://ssrn.com/abstract=1157158) Berkeley Business Law Journal, Vol. 6, No. 1, Spring 2009

[11] Martin, Andrew (January 4, 2010). "How Visa, Using Card Fees, Dominates a Market" (http://www.nytimes.com/2010/01/05/your-money/credit-and-debit-cards/05visa.html?em=&pagewanted=all). *New York Times*. . Retrieved 2010-01-06. "The fees, roughly 1 to 3 percent of each purchase, are forwarded to the cardholder's bank to cover costs and promote the issuance of more Visa cards."
[12] Dickler, Jessica (2008-07-31). "Hidden credit card fees are costing you" (http://money.cnn.com/2008/07/28/news/credit_card_interchange/). *CNN*. . Retrieved 2010-04-30.
[13] Carr, Ted (2010-09-02). "Minimizing Confusion Over Minimums" (http://blog.visa.com/2010/09/02/minimizing-confusion-over-minimums/). Blog.visa.com. . Retrieved 2011-07-28.
[14] http://mktsci.journal.informs.org/content/17/1/4
[15] http://moneyland.time.com/2011/07/07/finally-money-advice-that-will-make-you-skinnier/
[16] "Example of a supplement chargeable to the customer when paying by credit card" (http://www.bmibaby.com/bmibaby/terms_and_conditions/our_top_booking_tips,_baby/fees_and_charges.aspx). Bmibaby.com. 2011-01-05. . Retrieved 2011-07-28.
[17] "Credit Cards and You - About Pre-paid Cards" (http://web.archive.org/web/20070307084013/http://www.fcac-acfc.gc.ca/eng/publications/CreditCardsYou/PrepaidCards_e.asp). Financial Consumer Agency of Canada. Archived from the original (http://www.fcac-acfc.gc.ca/eng/publications/CreditCardsYou/PrepaidCards_e.asp) on 2007-03-07. . Retrieved 2008-01-09. document: "Pre-paid Cards" (http://web.archive.org/web/20080229122947/http://www.fcac-acfc.gc.ca/eng/publications/CreditCardsYou/PDFs/Prepaid-e.pdf) (PDF). Financial Consumer Agency of Canada. Archived from the original (http://www.fcac-acfc.gc.ca/eng/publications/CreditCardsYou/PDFs/Prepaid-e.pdf) on 2008-02-29. . Retrieved 2008-01-09.
[18] Secured Credit cards (http://www.fcac-acfc.gc.ca/eng/publications/CreditCardsYou/pdfs/Secured-e.pdf)
[19] "Buy prepaid credit cards without an ID or age limits? ... What could go wrong?" (http://www.networkworld.com/community/?q=node/11433). NetworkWorld.com Community
[20] FCAC launches pre-paid payment card guide (http://www.fcac-acfc.gc.ca/eng/media/news/default.asp?postingId=225)
[21] Pre-paid Cards (http://www.fcac.gc.ca/eng/publications/other/Prepaid/PDFs/Prepaid-eng.pdf)
[22] Thrive Business Solutions, http://www.thrivesolution.com/index.php?option=com_content&task=view&id=28&Itemid=33
[23] *Secure POS Vendor Alliance is launched by Hypercom, Ingenico and VeriFone* (http://www.ecommerce-journal.com/news/14854_secure_pos_vendor_alliance_is_launched_by_hypercom_ingenico_and_verifone). ECommerce Journal. 2009.
[24] Credit Card Issuer Fraud Management, Report Highlights, December, 2008 (http://www.sas.com/news/analysts/mercator_fraud_1208.pdf)
[25] Plastic fraud loss on UK-issued cards 2004/2005 (http://www.cardwatch.org.uk/media.asp?sectionid=4&pageid=109). Cardwatch.org.uk. site retrieved 7 July 2006
[26] United States Securities and Exchange Commission FORM S-1 (http://www.sec.gov/Archives/edgar/data/1403161/000119312507242653/ds1.htm), November 9, 2007.
[27] Debit Cards Cash In On Rewards Riches (http://www2.tbo.com/content/2008/feb/15/bz-debit-cards-cash-in-on-rewards-riches/) *Tampa Tribune*, Feb. 15, 2008.
[28] The Interchange Debate: Issues and Economics (http://www.minneapolisfed.org/pubs/region/06-06/interchange.cfm) James Lyon, Jan. 19, 2006
[29] Gracia, Mike (2008-05-09). "credit cards abroad" (http://www.creditchoices.co.uk/credit-card-charges-abroad.html). creditchoices.co.uk. . Retrieved 2008-05-09.
[30] "Comparison of exchange rates using Visa and Diners Club cards in Bali" (http://www.lonelyplanet.com/tonywheeler/my_lists/why_we_cut_up_our_credit_cards/). Lonelyplanet.com. 2010-03-03. . Retrieved 2011-07-28.
[31] "This is Money Card charges to be slashed" (http://www.thisismoney.co.uk/credit-and-loans/article.html?in_article_id=407583&in_page_id=9). Thisismoney.co.uk. 2006-03-13. . Retrieved 2011-07-28.
[32] "Current credit card default charges unfair" (http://www.oft.gov.uk/news/press/2006/68-06). Oft.gov.uk. . Retrieved 2011-07-28.
[33] FCAC - For Consumers - Interactive Tools - Credit Cards and You (http://www.fcac-acfc.gc.ca/eng/consumers/ITools/CreditCards/default.asp)
[34] National Center for Public Policy and Higher Education
[35] *CNN*. http://money.cnn.com/news/newsfeeds/articles/djf500/200712032215DOWJONESDJONLINE000777_FORTUNE5.htm.
[36] Joseph S. Enoch. "Credit Card Executives Tough Out Senate Hearing" (http://www.consumeraffairs.com/news04/2007/03/senate_credit_cards02.html). Consumeraffairs.com. . Retrieved 2011-07-28.
[37] "Statutory Instrument 1990 No. 2159: The Credit Cards (Price Discrimination) Order 1990" (http://www.opsi.gov.uk/si/si1990/Uksi_19902159_en_1.htm). Opsi.gov.uk. . Retrieved 2011-07-28.
[38] "Plastic cards in the UK and how we used them in 2007" (http://www.apacs.org.uk/resources_publications/card_facts_and_figures.html)
[39] American FactFinder, United States Census Bureau. "US Census: 2005–2007 American Community Survey 3-Year Estimates" (http://factfinder.census.gov/servlet/STTable?_bm=y&-geo_id=01000US&-qr_name=ACS_2007_3YR_G00_S0101&-ds_name=ACS_2007_3YR_G00_). Factfinder.census.gov. . Retrieved 2011-07-28.
[40] "Experian's National Score Index" (http://www.nationalscoreindex.com/ViewAllGraphs.aspx). Nationalscoreindex.com. . Retrieved 2011-07-28.
[41] "Prime Numbers: The Plastic Revolution" (http://www.foreignpolicy.com/story/cms.php?story_id=4207). Foreign Policy. 2008-02-19. . Retrieved 2011-07-28.

[42] "A start-up's true tale" (http://pdp10.nocrew.org/docs/cisco.html). Pdp10.nocrew.org. . Retrieved 2011-07-28.
[43] Google About Page under 1998 (http://www.google.com/intl/en/corporate/history.html) page retrieved 30 May 2007.
[44] Hollywood Shuffle trivia at IMDB (http://www.imdb.com/title/tt0093200/trivia) page retrieved 7 July 2006

External links

- Choosing A Credit Card: The Deal is in the Disclosures (http://www.ftc.gov/bcp/edu/pubs/consumer/credit/cre05.shtm) – Consumer credit card advice from the Federal Trade Commission
- Avoiding Credit and Charge Card Fraud (http://www.ftc.gov/bcp/edu/pubs/consumer/credit/cre07.shtm) – More advice from the Federal Trade Commission
- Credit Cards (http://www.dmoz.org/Business/Financial_Services/Banking_Services/Credit_Cards/) at the Open Directory Project

Investment

Investment has different meanings in finance and economics. Finance investment is putting money into something with the expectation of gain, that upon thorough analysis, has a high degree of security for the principal amount, as well as security of return, within an expected period of time.[1] In contrast putting money into something with an expectation of gain without thorough analysis, without security of principal, and without security of return is speculation or gambling.

Investment is related to saving or deferring consumption. Investment is involved in many areas of the economy, such as business management and finance whether for households, firms, or governments.

To avoid speculation an investment must be either directly backed by the pledge of sufficient collateral or insured by sufficient assets pledged by a third party. A thoroughly analyzed loan of money backed by collateral with greater immediate value than the loan amount may be considered an investment. A financial instrument that is insured by the pledge of assets from a third party, such as a deposit in a financial institution insured by a government agency may be considered an investment. Examples of these agencies include, in the United States, the Securities Investor Protection Corporation, Federal Deposit Insurance Corporation, or National Credit Union Administration, or in Canada, the Canada Deposit Insurance Corporation.

Promoters of and news sources that report on speculative financial transactions such as stocks, mutual funds, real estate, oil and gas leases, commodities, and futures often inaccurately or misleadingly describe speculative schemes as investment.

Investment: thorough analysis and security. Speculation: analysis and some risk. Gambling: lack of analysis and lack of safety.

In economics or macroeconomics

In economic theory or in macroeconomics, investment is the amount purchased per unit time of goods which are not consumed but are to be used for future production. Examples include railroad or factory construction. Investment in human capital includes costs of additional schooling or on-the-job training. Inventory investment refers to the accumulation of goods inventories; it can be positive or negative, and it can be intended or unintended. In measures of national income and output, "gross investment" (represented by the variable I) is also a component of Gross domestic product (GDP), given in the formula GDP = C + I + G + NX, where C is consumption, G is government spending, and NX is net exports. Thus investment is everything that remains of total expenditure after consumption, government spending, and net exports are subtracted (i.e. I = GDP - C - G - NX).

Non-residential fixed investment (such as new factories) and residential investment (new houses) combine with inventory investment to make up I. "Net investment" deducts depreciation from gross investment. Net fixed investment is the value of the net increase in the capital stock per year.

Fixed investment, as expenditure over a period of time ("per year"), is not capital. The time dimension of investment makes it a *flow*. By contrast, capital is a *stock*— that is, accumulated net investment *to a point* in time (such as December 31).

Investment is often modeled as a function of Income and Interest rates, given by the relation I = f(Y, r). An increase in income encourages higher investment, whereas a higher interest rate may discourage investment as it becomes more costly to borrow money. Even if a firm chooses to use its own funds in an investment, the interest rate represents an opportunity cost of investing those funds rather than lending out that amount of money for interest.[2]

Investment related to business of a firm - business management

The investment decision (also known as capital budgeting) is one of the fundamental decisions of business management: Managers determine the investment value of the assets that a business enterprise has within its control or possession. These assets may be physical (such as buildings or machinery), intangible (such as patents, software, goodwill), or financial (see below). Assets are used to produce streams of revenue that often are associated with particular costs or outflows. All together, the manager must determine whether the net present value of the investment to the enterprise is positive using the marginal cost of capital that is associated with the particular area of business.

In terms of financial assets, these are often marketable securities such as a company stock (an equity investment) or bonds (a debt investment). At times, the goal of the investment is to produce future cash flows, while at others it may be for the purpose of gaining access to more assets by establishing control or influence over the operation of a second company (the investee).

Business firms or organisations raise funds from investors in the form of equites and debts (collectively known as the capital structure) and further reinvest it into various investment schemes by carefully analysing the returns in order to meet out their obligations relating to purchase of assets which provides them long term benefits.

In finance

In finance, investment is the commitment of funds through collateralized lending, or making a deposit into a secured institution.

In contrast to investment; dollar cost averaging, market timing, and diversification are phrases associated with speculation.

Investments are often made indirectly through intermediaries, such as banks, Credit Unions, Brokers, Lenders, and insurance companies. Though their legal and procedural details differ, an intermediary generally makes an investment using money from many individuals, each of whom receives a claim on the intermediary.

History

The Code of Hammurabi 1700 B.C. provided a legal framework for investment establishing a means for the pledge of collateral by codifying debtor and creditor rights in regard to pledged land. Punishments for breaking financial obligations were not as severe as those for crimes involving injury or death.

In the early 1900s purchasers of stocks, bonds, and other securities were described in media, academia, and commerce as speculators. By the 1950s the term investment had been co-opted by financial brokers and their advertising agencies to promote speculation.

Linguistic significance

Common usage of "investment" to describe "speculation" has reduced investor capacity to discern investment from speculation, reduced investor awareness of risk associated with speculation, increased capital available to speculation, and decreased capital available to investment.

Real estate as the instrument of investment

In real estate, investment money is used to purchase property for the purpose of holding, reselling or leasing for income and there is an element of capital risk.

Residential real estate

Investment in residential real estate is the most common form of real estate investment measured by number of participants because it includes property purchased as a primary residence. In many cases the buyer does not have the full purchase price for a property and must engage a lender such as a bank, finance company or private lender. Different countries have their individual normal lending levels, but usually they will fall into the range of 70-90% of the purchase price. Against other types of real estate, residential real estate is the least risky.

Commercial real estate

Commercial real estate consists of multifamily apartments, office buildings, retail space, hotels and motels, warehouses, and other commercial properties. Due to the higher risk of commercial real estate, loan-to-value ratios allowed by banks and other lenders are lower and often fall in the range of 50-70%.

See also

- Asset
- Speculation
- Risk
- Alternative investments
- Diversifying investment
- Foreign direct investment
- List of countries by gross fixed investment as percentage of GDP
- List of economics topics
- Mortgage Investment Corporation
- Rate of return (ROR, a.k.a. ROI)
- Socially responsible investing
- Specialized investment fund

Notes

[1] Graham, Benjamin and David Dodd (1951). *Security Analysis*. McGraw-Hill Book Comany. ISBN 007144829.

[2] Kevin A. Hassett (2008, 2nd ed.). "Investment," (http://www.econlib.org/library/Enc/Investment.html) *The Concise Encyclopedia of Economics*. Library of Economics and Liberty.

External links

- Investing (http://www.dmoz.org/Business/Investing/Stocks_and_Bonds/Equities/Research_and_Analysis//) at the Open Directory Project

Article Sources and Contributors

Security Service Federal Credit Union *Source*: http://en.wikipedia.org/w/index.php?title=Security_Service_Federal_Credit_Union *Contributors*: Dpfitzen, Gobonobo, LilHelpa, Maqsarian, OccamzRazor, Pawyilee, Pearrari, R'n'B, Rjwilmsi, Sahrin, Steveotx1, TexasAndroid, Xnatedawgx, Ylem, 24 anonymous edits

Natural person *Source*: http://en.wikipedia.org/w/index.php?title=Natural_person *Contributors*: Apokrif, Arthena, Bhuston, BoNoMoJo (old), Brewcrewer, Bulatych, Chaojoker, Charles Matthews, ClaesWallin, D, D3gtrd, David.Monniaux, Dcstamm, DocWatson42, Dreftymac, Eastlaw, Estevoaei, Evercat, Fvasconcellos, Gary King, Gregzeng, Howcheng, Inkling, JHMM13, Keilana, Ksyrie, Lucy-marie, M.R.B., Mac, Maximilian2010, Michael Hardy, Mindmatrix, Miss Mondegreen, Montrealais, Mormegil, Nick Carraway, Notorious4life, Pakaran, Physicistjedi, Puckly, Reinis, Skakkle, Suradnik13, Vedek Dukat, Waacstats, Wayiran, Why My Fleece?, 42 anonymous edits

Credit union *Source*: http://en.wikipedia.org/w/index.php?title=Credit_union *Contributors*: 1101701010, 72Dino, 84user, Adolfo29, Ahmed badda, Alphathon, AmishThrasher, Andres, AndySimpson, Appeltree1, Ariel., ArtChamb, Barek, Bazj, Bearcat, Ben MacDui, Bensaccount, Bertman, Bevo, Biederman, Bigbluefish, BillBell, Bomfog, Bouchecl, Bradrose90, Brett epic, Buybooks Marius, CUguy, Calabe1992, Calicat, Cardsplayer4life, Cflm001, Childepm, Chiptrimmier, Chris Lincoln, Ciaran.mooney, Click23, Cmorris13, Commander Keane, Creditunionist, Cybercobra, Cyrie, DBaba, DV8 2XL, Dale Arnett, DaughterofSun, DavidLevinson, Dhkermit, Djegan, Doborjginidze, DocendoDiscimus, Drewwiki, Dubc0724, Duine Aosta, EPM, Eastlaw, Edward, Elwood j blues, Erud, F15 sanitizing eagle, Falcon Kirtaran, Falcon8765, Feedmecereal, Femto, Fish and karate, FisherQueen, FrancisTyers, FreplySpang, Friejose, Gaius Cornelius, Gavin.collins, Giraffedata, Gmorishige, Gobonobo, Gowish, Granwagschal, Gregalton, Gshurley, Guajero, Gwernol, Historian932, Hroðulf, IanMcGreene, Iktae, Indeterminate, Isaf jones, Itsmejudith, J.delanoy, JSchroth, Jeffq, JeremyA, JimMillerJr, John Quiggin, Johnhold, Johnsbone, Jonathan.s.kt, Jsayre64, Jstreutker, Juanaguas, K. Annoyomous, KGasso, Kariteh, Katieh5584, Ken Gallager, Killian441, Kingturtle, Kinou, KnowledgeOfSelf, KowDude, Larrypaulb, Lavenderbunny, Lethargy, Lexi Marie, Lowaystar, Ltmesq, M@sk, Manop, Manshuv, Mathieugp, Mbiama Assogo Roger, Mediaimages, Mfield, Mic, Michael93555, Michaelbarr123, Miffy900, Mikel1777, Mmpartee, Momo san, Monty845, MoriyaMinakata, MrVoluntarist, Mwanner, Ncmattj, Noah Salzman, Notheruser, Nposs, Olaffpomona, Orayzio, Parande, Paul Stansifer, Paulburnett, Pearrari, Peruvianllama, Peter Clarke, Petri Krohn, Pgan002, Pgreenfinch, Phatom87, Plastikspork, Pmb2397, Polpo, Puuma21, Quidam65, RaffyO, Rfc1394, Ribeyed, RingtailedFox, Rjwilmsi, Robert1947, RockyRaccoon, Rodsan18, Rogklein, Roleplayer, Rommyappus, Rttd411, Ryulong, Sam8, SchuminWeb, Scott Sanchez, Sherurcij, Shii, SimonP, SiobhanHansa, Sjakkalle, SkerHawx, Skoblentz, Smallman12q, Smbroad, Specious, Stepheng3, Stormie, Superbuddha, Taffenzee, Teilolondon, Terrypin, Thumperward, Timc, Tox, Vegaswikian, Verne Equinox, Vincentl, Voyager640, Wahiba, Wavelength, What does it mean to you, Wiki emma johnson, Williamkilgore, Witzenburg, Wnzrf, X!, Yellow Element, 298 anonymous edits

San Antonio *Source*: http://en.wikipedia.org/w/index.php?title=San_Antonio *Contributors*: .marc., 08OceanBeach SD, 11tas, 123home123, 13montel, 16@r, 1958publius, 1fatkat4u, 25or6to4, 28421u2232nfenfcenc, A. B., A1a2b3, ABF, AFI2003, AQUIMISMO, Abhishekofmadras, Academic Challenger, Acalamari, Acather96, Acntx, AdamJacobMuller, Addison0426, Aequo, Ageekgal, Ahoerstemeier, Ahuskay, Aitias, Alamocitydotcom, Alamotours, Alan Liefting, Alansohn, Alcal1, AlexAndAaron, AlexCovarrubias, AlexiusHoratius, Alexjon, Amazonien, Ambyent, Amreatsf4620, Anclation, Andershalden, AndirisAiyya, Andrewcool, Andy Marchbanks, Angr, AnmaFinotera, Anonymous Dissident, Another Believer, Appraiser, Arch dude, Artemis3120, Aruton, Asocall, Astuishin, Atlantabravz, Aude, August Dominus, Auntof6, Austin273, Ayla, B4hand, BD2412, BLT, Barfooz, Basar, Bbailey51, Belovedfreak, Bender235, Bentley4, Benwbrum, Bgdigital, Bigred43, Billy Hathorn, Birdhunter, Bleh999, Blu.wyte, BlueAg09, Blugu64, Bob frasier, Bobblewik, Bobby H. Heffley, Bobdud56, Bobo192, Boothy443, Bordadores, BorisG, Bovineone, Brandon1978, BrandonR, Brianreading, Brownings, Btgervais, Buffs, Buthole4, Butros, ButterflyMom21, CalebNoble, Calvin 1998, Can't sleep, clown will eat me, Canadaolympic989, Cantiorix, Cape cod naturalist, Capricorn42, Captureme5117, Carbonix, Carlosguitar, Carlossuarez46, Carptrash, Cbrillson, Cbustapeck, Cdman882, Cfrancis, Charou, CheepnisAroma, ChevyNazi, Chimeraweaver, Chnou, Chowbok, Chr.K., Chrishmt0423, Chrislk02, Cleared as filed, Clinton350, Clipper471, Cmc0, Cmdrjameson, Cntras, Coemgenus, Cohee, CommonsDelinker, Concan5, Conscious, Cool Stuff Is Cool, Cool3, CoolMan2000, Corey Grandy, Corpjet92, Corpx, Cougarspride, CrazyC83, Creator7, Cretanforever, Cst17, Csyberblue, Ctjf83, Custodisverum, Cyrus Andiron, Cyrusc, D Marc, D6, DARTH SIDIOUS 2, DIDouglass, DLS Texas, DS1953, Dabomb87, Daltnpapi4u, Dan100, Daniel Olsen, Danman111111, Dannyking@wikipedia.org, Darren Jowalsen, Darth Panda, Darwinek, Dave6, Davefulp, David009, DavidLevinson, Dcampion, Dcoetzee, Debresser, Deflective, Dekisugi, Delldot, DemocraticLuntz, Dennis Brown, Deor, Derek.cashman, Derekmarc, Dfrt5, Dhdez05, Dionysostom, Diplomacy Guy, Dknights411, DocWatson42, Donald Albury, DoubleBlue, Doug, Download, Downwards, Dr31, Dravecky, Droll, Drumguy8800, Duz, Dylan620, E. Sn0 =31337=, ERK, ESQ24, EagleFan, Eco84, Ed g2s, Edderso, Edkiii, Edpsychdoc1, Efe, Eleventhhour, Elias Chavez, Elizabeth705, Eluchil404, Emmc5, Emoll, Emurph, Epbr123, Erebus555, Ericdn, Es330td, EugeneZelenko, Evans1982, Extransit, Extraordinary Machine, Falcon8765, FastLizard4, Fastily, Fieldday-sunday, Firsfron, FloppyDiskMan, Flurgleflurgle, Flyingimc23, FrankCostanza, Fratrep, Frescavergene, Fritz Saalfeld, Froid, Fshoutofdawater, Fsmatovu, Fundamental metric tensor, Funnyhat, Fuzzy510, G. Capo, GETONERD84, GHe, Gabedomia, Gabefarkas, Gaius Cornelius, Galwhaa, Gamaliel, Gary King, Gateman1997, GeoGreg, Geologyguy, Gerry D, Gfoley4, Ggretser, Giants27, Giftlite, Giraffedata, Gocontributor, Gogo Dodo, Golbez, Graham87, Gray Spot, Greenshed, Griffinofwales, Groselab, Ground Zero, Grubbmeister, GuidoGuanz, Gymgirl995, H8risin, HastEggqui, HennessyC, Hephaestos, HighlyEvolved, Highlycaffeinated, Holdercal, Holidayking, Hoopsguy98, Howcheng, Hpav7, Hugh16, Huhwaitwhoareyou, Iam emperor, Ian Pitchford, Ianjones50, Iarescientists, Icebrg, Ichabod, Idont Havaname, Igoldste, InNotOf395, Infrogmation, Iridescent, Island Monkey, Isnapm, Ixfd64, J rosales1, J. Spencer, J.Hawthorne, J.delanoy, JCarriker, JForget, JFreeman, JHawk88, JRC1285, Jaga185, Jardinessardine, Jasonjrb, Jatkins, Jatoria, Java7837, Jay Litman, Jaysscholar, Jck2007, Jdscotttx, Jecowa, Jeff G., Jenn Dolari, JeremyA, Jerome Charles Potts, JetBlast, Jfitts, Jfknrh, Jhendin, Jinpendragon, Jllm06, Jmaddux23, Joaquin008, JodyB, JoeSmack, Joelfromhell, John of Reading, Jon Alten, Jonathan.s.kt, Jorge21o, Joseph Solis in Australia, JoshCerda, Joy, Jpinsatx, Jpwashere, Jt8185, Jugni, Junafani, Jusdafax, Justbarbour, Justinah, Justinah88, Jw 193, Kaldari, Kaszeta, Kat Malone, Kaushikmechano, Kbdank71, Kcranson, Ke2150, Kendrick7, Kettleworks, Kewp, Kharker, Khfamily, Kibinsky, Kilmas565, King of Hearts, Kingpin13, Kinneyboy90, Kkinder, Kkmd, KnowledgeOfSelf, Koavf, Kramada, Kramden4700, Kransky, Krellis, Krushsister, Ktr101, Kumar Appaiah, Kuru, Kurykh, Kwamikagami, Kyr-Roger deM, L Kensington, La Pianista, Lakekirby, Laplush225, LarryHoward, Latitude0116, Laurelrogers, LawerenceSmit, LeeG, Leuko, Levineps, Lhall, Lightmouse, Ligulem, LilHelpa, LinguistAtLarge, Little Mountain 5, LittleOldMe, LlywelynII, Loadmaster, Local hero, Lockley, LonelyMarble, Longhornsguy07, Loodog, Lordthorpez, Luk, Lynnell, M5891, MBisanz, MER-C, MJCdetroit, MK8, MP123, Magog the Ogre, Magusdee, Majormadmax, Mallxx, Manderiko, Marcobarros, Marek69, Mariordo, Markcamann, Markeross, Marriedtofilm, Mateo SA, Materialscientist, Mathpianist93, Mattbr, Matthewgarth, MattieTK, Mattscards, Maverick9711, Mcorazao, Mes tex, Miaht82, Mikebrand, Mild Bill Hiccup, MindscapesGraphicDesign, Miranda, Mircea cs, MirelesJ, Mjay1120, Mlaffs, Mm40, Moncrief, Monterey Bay, Moreau36, Mosmof, Mphifer254, Mr. Ash, Msh210, Mtt124, Myanw, NE2, Nahallac Silverwinds, Naniwako, NastyBob, NawlinWiki, Neural, Neutrality, Nightryder84, Niichnichelle, Noformation, NorthernFire, Notdedyet, Nuevec, Nuno Tavares, Nv8200p, Nyttend, Ocatecir, Ohnoitsjamie, Okiefromokla (old), Oldag07, Oldmanshirt, Orthographer, Oxymoron83, P.o.h, P870101, PBP, Pacaro, PattonZarate, Paulscott, Peace01234, Pepper, Peruvianllama, Petrichor, Philip Baird Shearer, Philip Trueman, Piano non troppo, Pinkadelica, Pladask, Plasma Twa 2, PleaseStand, Polaron, Pooleyusk, Popegeorgeringo, Postoak, Prevod&priredba, Prufrock1, Purgatory Fubar, QcolorRed, Quidam65, Quota, R, R5H4D0W, RG2, RJN, RSM, Ra59456, Raider042678, Ralphwiggam75, Ram-Man, Rannpháirtí anaithnid, Rayasmith, Raymata1, Realaudio2007, Reba d, Recordco, Red245, Redrocket, Reezy, Revth, RexNL, Rhatsa26X, Rhrad, Rich Farmbrough, Richie, Rick.Wicks, Rifleman 82, Riparks, Riverwalk, Rjwilmsi, Rlbarton, Rnieves1977, Robomaeyhem, Rocker094, Rockhopper10r, Rocksanne, Ronhjones, Ronz, Ropratt, Rumping, Runmiler429, Rwalker, Ryanbodnar, Ryanheward, Rylee118, Ryoung122, SNIyer12, Sabresareking23, Sahmeditor, Sahrin, Salty!, Samba6566, Sami99tr, Sampo Torgo, Sanantoniochamber, Sandia seed, Saracarl, Sbmeirow, SchfiftyThree, Schwenk182, Scm83x, ScottDavis, Scotthatton, Sdowlatshahi, Sean WI, Searchme, Sedna10387, SelfStudyBuddy, Sersarsor, Seth Ilys, Several Times, Sfear, Sfrers, Shabooooom, Shannnnnnnt, Shereth, Shirt58, Sidfoo, Sir, Sizzlersteak, Sjsharksrs, Skiboarder6730, Sligocki, Smallbones, Smith120bh, Snowolf, Sohailstyle, SoiAdmin, SoundGod3, South Bay, SpaceFlight89, SpanishCastleMagic, Stallex, Stallions2010, Stefanomione, Stephenb, Stern, Steveozone, Stmarystx, Storm Rider, Streetlightsbadnews, Strovanman, SugarPlum, Supine, Sw258, Synchronism, TBM10, THEN WHO WAS PHONE?, THEPLANETEARTH, TMS63112, TRBP, Tampasteve, Tanktimus, Tbone762, Tedernst, Template namespace initialisation script, TenOfAllTrades, Tenticle, Teratornis, Texas2752, TexasAndroid, Texasreb, The Thing That Should Not Be, The Universe Is Cool, TheLastAmigo, TheNewPhobia, Thehopecreed, Thorncrag, Tibetan Prayer, Tiddly Tom, Tide rolls, TimRoe1203, Timelock, Tlytkine, Tom Danson, Tom harrison, TonyTheTiger, Tophernino, Tpbradbury, Trasman, Travuun, Trovatore, Turian, Two PhDs and a Master's Degree, Twpcru123, UH Collegian, Ufwuct, Unity77, Uris, User86654, Vanka5, Vegas cat, Vegaswikian, Ventusa, Versus22, Vespuccia, Voyagerfan5761, VsevolodKrolikov, Wapcaplet, Webaware, Werdan7, WereSpielChequers, WhisperToMe, Wik, Wikipedian2, WillC, Willconsuegra, William Allen Simpson, WilliamSven, Willking1979, Wimt, Witchking111111, Wmahan, Woohookitty, WriterHound, Wtmitchell, Wwoods, XPTO, XxTrillvillexX9, Ybbor, YellowMonkey, Yewlongbow, Yk Yk Yk, Yumyumchicken, Zahid Abdassabur, Zereshk, Zerofoks, Zoicon5, Zzyzx11, Δ, A, شرزر, 1763 anonymous edits

South Texas *Source*: http://en.wikipedia.org/w/index.php?title=South_Texas *Contributors*: AMAPO, Acalamari, Acntx, Aitias, Alai, Allen3, Aristophanes68, Atownballer, Blub, Bovlb, Caknuck, CaptainJae, ChrisCork, Cobra libre, Col. Kernal, CommonsDelinker, Crlittle1, Danny5007, DarkElite239, Dcampion, Dennis Brown, Dough4872, El Krem, Fingers-of-Pyrex, FisherQueen, Frecklefoot, FredR, Gogo Dodo, Grutness, Hike395, Hmains, Hooperswim, JCarriker, JamesAM, Joseph Solis in Australia, Lawikitejana, Letoofdune, LilHelpa, Limideen, LonelyMarble, Maile66, Nononsenseplease, Pearle, ProudTexasCitizen, R'n'B, RJN, RandySavageFTW, Rjh602, Simesa, Smokey2, Sortior, Stallions2010, Thebeginning, WhisperToMe, William Saturn, Wizardman, Woohookitty, Zephyrnthesky, 110 anonymous edits

Savings account *Source*: http://en.wikipedia.org/w/index.php?title=Savings_account *Contributors*: A8UDI, Airodyssey, Alansohn, Allforfree, Angr, Arcenciel, Bloodshedder, Bluedaimond, Bobblehead, Bunchofgrapes, Calwatch, Cmichael, Cww, DGJM, DanMatan, David Gale, Dcandeto, DocendoDiscimus, Doldrums, Dylan Lake, Eastlaw, Effan, Emurphy42, Finnand80, Furrykef, GeezusChryste, Gregbard, Gwernol, Hbent, Hersfold, Hroðulf, IRP, Ike9898, J.delanoy, Jenova20, Jerryseinfeld, Jkeene, Joel7687, Jwoodger, KnowledgeOfSelf, Kukini, Kuru, Longhair, Loonymonkey, Markber, Matt Deres, Maurreen, Mbarra, Michfan2123, MrC539, Ohnoitsjamie, Oscarthecat, Pakaran, Petri Krohn, Philip Trueman, Pnm, Propaniac, Qwghlm, Qxz, Rabsnieder, Rdsmith4, Redmarkviolinist, Roadrunner, Rrburke, Sheeana, Shirik, Sicherlich, Signalhead, Silivrenion, Simon123, Small Bug, SmthManly, Some jerk on the Internet, Someones life, Sonic da hedgehog, South Bay, Stephenb, TAG.Odessa, Timetolearn, Tordek ar, Train2104, W.Kaleem, Whisky drinker, Wkfswebmistress, Yekwah, Zvis, 221 anonymous edits

Transactional account *Source*: http://en.wikipedia.org/w/index.php?title=Transactional_account *Contributors*: Airodyssey, Alansohn, Alex.johnson, Amitauti, Antandrus, Arthena, Atyphoon, Barts1a, Bora52, Bradgib, Brentdax, Camtra1, CanisRufus, Ckatz, Cranialsodomy, Crusnik117, DJ Clayworth, Davish Krail, Gold Five, Delldot, DerHexer, Discospinster, DocWatson42, DocendoDiscimus, Dominic, Doughyden, Eastlaw, Edward, Elurian, Eyreland, Fishnet37222, Fresheneesz, Fwc, Greensburger, HDCase, Hairy Dude, Hydrox, Ian3055, Imnotminkus, Improv,

Ishikawa Minoru, JaGa, JackLumber, Jackeapen, Jag123, Jasondmath, Jclemens, Jeff G., Jeffq, Jeretad, Jerryseinfeld, Jezebel280, Jorfer, Kazanma, Khfan93, Klip game, Krawi, Lotje, MaCRoEco, MadScientistMatt, Maho4905, Markber, Markseibert, Materialscientist, Mkweise, Mradigan, Msleeth, Nbarth, Netalarm, Nwbeeson, Ohnoitsjamie, Omegatron, Oswald Glinkmeyer, Peilan, Petri Krohn, Pip2andahalf, Pnm, Prashanthns, RevTenderBranson, Rfc1394, Roadrunner, Sargdub, Simon123, SimonTrew, SirBob42, Someguy1221, Srleffler, The Thing That Should Not Be, TrbleClef, Uncle-P, Vuong Ngan Ha, Wiki Raja, Wjejskenewr, Wkfswebmistress, Xandi, 138 anonymous edits

Loan *Source*: http://en.wikipedia.org/w/index.php?title=Loan *Contributors*: 21655, A. B., AThing, Adamou166, AdjustShift, Airodyssey, Ajg1981, Alansohn, AlistairMcMillan, Altenmann, Andres, Andrinawilson12, Antonio Lopez, Aoi, Arcadie, Astronautics, Avicennasis, Ayrton Prost, BD2412, Babygirl90, Badmash007, Barticus88, Becritical, Bedivere, Belmond, Bhadani, Biker Biker, Bobcollins2, Bongwarrior, Brad whitehead, Bradmca, Brim, Cacycle, Callofduty007, Can't sleep, clown will eat me, CanadianPenguin, Carloancanada, Cent-Hero, Chrisch, CliffC, Cmcgurran84, Connie937, Creditplus, Creditsource, Cww, Danarmstrong, Davey.gold, David4286, Dazzledandconfused, Dcoetzee, Dee10dee, Deleteme42, Df53515, Diannaa, Dina, Discospinster, Dlohcierekim's sock, Dmeyerstax, DocendoDiscimus, Dominic, Drumbum, Dysprosia, E-citizen, Ekowasan, El C, Ergative rlt, Eugene van der Pijll, Eukesh, Ewlyahoocom, Falcon8765, Fastilysock, Favonian, Feco, Fenice, Financeinfo, Firsfron, Forexmaster, FrancoGG, Fredrik, GRBerry, Gaius Cornelius, Gioto, GraemeL, Grafen, Gregalton, Gurch, Gwernol, Hadal, HaeB, Harry, Hede2000, Hellorere, HorsePunchKid, I already forgot, ILuvTea, Idleguy, Igoldste, ImperfectlyInformed, Indon, J.delanoy, J0lt C0la, Japanese Searobin, Jasondmath, Jasonschnarr, Jeepday, Jemens, Jennifermaben, Jkeene, Jocandle, Jojoy, Jokinen, JorgeS, Jp 223, Jpd23, Karembo, Kasreyn, Keith27, King of Hearts, KuroiShiroi, Kuru, Laptop.graham, Leanellevera, Leebo, Leinadnav, Levineps, Linkspamremover, Livajo, Loanagreement, Lradrama, Luna Santin, MER-C, Mac, Macrakis, Mailtoramkumar, MaineRoamer, Marc Venot, Margapierre, Mark272, Martin Jensen, Maurreen, Mav, Maximus Rex, Mic, Misterx2000, MithrandirAgain, Monkeyman, Mortgages1, MrJones, Mvpsworld, Mydogategodshat, Myjoshuatree, Naive rm, NawlinWiki, Nbarth, Nepenthes, Nick, Nirvana2013, Nlu, NoPetrol, Nopetro, Notinasnaid, Numbo3, Obeaudel, Odie5533, OffsBlink, Ohconfucius, Ohnoitsjamie, Ojay123, Olaffpomona, Oswegobag, Pascal.Tesson, Patrick, Pero Despotovic, Persiana, Petteri Aimonen, Phgao, Philip Trueman, Plastikspork, Pne, Pnm, Pradeepg19, Psb777, QRX, Rasmus Faber, Ratirajkumar, Reaper Eternal, RedHillian, Reinyday, Reonwaterman, Rhobite, Richard L. Peterson, Rising*From*Ashes, Robert Merkel, Romeo3000, Rosser1954, Rror, SJP, SWAdair, Samchau94, Sasquatch, SchfiftyThree, Serg!o, Shadowdrak, Sherley19, SimonP, Stephenb, Suffusion of Yellow, Synchronism, TKD, Taffenzee, Taxman, Templatehater, Texture, The Thing That Should Not Be, TheMortgageMen, Thinking of England, Tide rolls, TigerShark, Tintazul, Tombomp, Tptrillion, Trekk, Trusilver, Tyrol5, Ucanlookitup, Uncle Dick, Uncle G, UninvitedCompany, Urbanrenewal, Usuchamp, Uthbrian, VV10elc, Vantala, Vesalr, VigilantPenguin, Wikibofh, Wmahan, Wolfman, Woohookitty, Xeno, Yankees76, Yidisheryid, Yonidebest, Yummifruitbat, ZimZalaBim, Zzuuzz, 484 anonymous edits

Mortgage loan *Source*: http://en.wikipedia.org/w/index.php?title=Mortgage_loan *Contributors*: 100 Mortgage, 102orion, Affihq, Akula83, Alansohn, Alsandro, Altenmann, Andy Dingley, Andyjsmith, Arsene, BD2412, Banker0679, Barek, Barticus88, Bettia, Bisti89, Calvinwalker, Canadarates, Carlmclean, Cent-Hero, Chrishaw, Ckatz, Clicketyclack, Cojo49, Craigballhagen, Crisisdebt, Crystalbeard, Cynical, DARTH SIDIOUS 2, Danorton, Dawnseeker2000, Denisarona, Discussall, Doc9871, DoriSmith, Download, Dowtel, Drmies, Eleazar, Emmalulu, Espoo, Evilknny9, Excirial, Fakie540, Favonian, Firestitch, Flowanda, Forexmaster, Funandtrvl, Funnyfarmofdoom, GB fan, Gary King, Gbscomp, Gilbertryan, Giraffedata, Gogo Dodo, Goodnightmush, Grafen, Gregalton, Ground Zero, Guoguo12, Haethos, Hedgehog41, Hmains, IRP, ImperfectlyInformed, Int21h, Isolation booth, JForget, JHP, JNW, Jakas1, Janjua786, Jaykeating, Jimbwayne, Joseph Solis in Australia, Jrtayloriv, Jusdafax, KamuiShirou, Katanada, Kayau, Kummi, Kuru, Kwertii, LaidOff, Laptop.graham, Luk, Lumbercutter, Mack7, Malhonen, Mathdeveloper, Melvinthegreat, Mianchen, MikeHammer, Mikek836, Minhoba, Mookie-wk, Mostpop, Murrax, Noelkoutlis, Notinasnaid, Nsevs, Nylis, Ohnoitsjamie, Open2universe, Orbital fox, Orgage, Ouroboros79, Paste, Piano non troppo, Pinethicket, Pnm, Polygon4, Pringati singarimbun, Proactivity, Prokopenya Viktor, Promethean, Quest for Truth, Qwfp, R'n'B, Radio Guy, Rahul Paeek, Rasmus Faber, Razorflame, Rd232, Reach Out to the Truth, Redquark, Rhubarb27, Robert Weemeyer, Rrburke, Ruhbee!, S Marshall, SCFilm29, Sabrina1973, Sardanaphalus, Scientus, Sciprogrammer, Scratchweasel, Shattered, Simon123, SiobhanHansa, Spiel, SueHay, Survtime, Taymoss, Techman224, Teles, Tgeairn, Todd Vierling, Tonypandyja, Transkey, Triwbe, Versageek, Vrenator, WPArgentarius, Wickerman45, Woohookitty, Yahel Guhan, Yanniraz, Yilloslime, Ysfcapricorn, Zubeco, Zzuuzz, Սահակ, 233 anonymous edits

Credit card *Source*: http://en.wikipedia.org/w/index.php?title=Credit_card *Contributors*: 16@r, 2eet2eet, 4twenty42o, 72Dino, A little insignificant, A. B., A.Z., A2swimmer, ABF, ARC Gritt, Aarondonaghy, Aaronw, AbJ32, Academic Challenger, Acrazy007, Acroterion, Adam Thomsett, Adam2288, Adam850, Adw2000, After Midnight, Ageekgal, Agrahlma, Ahoerstemeier, Ahsee.khan, Airodyssey, Aitias, Akamad, Alansohn, Albedo, Albert Gonzalez, Alblefter, Aleo1203, AlexJ, Alipur7, Allstarecho, Altenmann, Amatulic, Ameliorate!, Americans, AmiDaniel, Amitchakraborty, Anders94, Andrewpmk, Angletara, Animum, Annmed, Anon lynx, Antandrus, Anvilx, Apoc2400, Appleseed, Ardonik, Are you ready for IPv6?, ArielGold, Arvinder.virk, Arwel Parry, Asbestos, Ashwyns, Asparagus, AussieDingo1983, Avatar, Avidiax, AxelBoldt, Ayfi, Az29, AzaToth, BD2412, BIL, BRUTE, Babakathy, Backslash Forwardslash, Bama9205, Barneyboo, Baylink, Bcostley, Bearnfæder, Bearsharexx, Beetstra, Beland, BenFrantzDale, Benbest, BergZ, Berkut, Betacommand, Bettia, Bg, Bhadani, Bharatcit, BiT, Bilbito, Blahma, Bluemoose, Bobo192, Bobqwe, Bodnotbod, Boing! said Zebedee, Bonadea, Bongwarrior, BrainMagMo, Bramude, Branton, Bsartre, Bucketsofg, Buckinghampalace101, Buddha24, Burntsauce, Busiken, Butko, Buzlighty1, C.Fred, CL, CMG, CTZMSC3, CWenger, CWii, Cab88, Cahk, Calabe1992, Callcredit, Calmer Waters, Caltas, Can't sleep, clown will eat me, CanadianOne, CanisRufus, Canrocks, Capricorn42, Caramesc, Casmith 789, Catamorphism, Cazort, Ccnj, Ccuenca11, CesarB, Ceyockey, Cha ching24, Chairsenses, Chanakal, CharlotteWebb, Chasingsol, Chealer, Choosid, Chowbok, Chris Donnelly, Chris1123, Chrisbrl88, Chubbles, ChubbyLumpkins, Ckape, Clawed, Clearpay, Clepbooks, Cliffb, Cluth, Cntras, Cocoromania, Cod lord, Coffee, Cokoli, Collinlc, Cometstyles, CommonsDelinker, Computerjoe, Coneslayer, Cooksey, Coolcaesar, CopperMurdoch, Cpl Syx, Cralar, Creditsource, Cremepuff222, Crickel, Crisjoy1996, Crobb305, Crocodile Punter, Crunchy Numbers, Cute 1 4 u, Cymru.lass, Cynical, Czj, Da Joe, Daleyj, Damian Yerrick, Daniel5127, Dark jedi requiem, David.Monniaux, DavidCiani, Dawn Bard, Dcandeto, Dekisugi, Deli nk, Delirium, Delldot, DeltaQuad, DemonLordTyrus, DerHexer, Desideal, Desinlabor3, Dforest, Dhev ijaya20, Diamonte, Digitalme, Discospinster, Dlohcierekim, DocWatson42, DocendoDiscimus, Dominus, Donarreiskoffer, Dondon83, Doniago, Donreed, DrHydeous, Drc79, Dreamword, Dross82, Dsdukcy, Duagloth, Dulciana, Dylan Lake, Dysanovic, Dysprosia, Dzfoo, EEPROM Eagle, ERcheck, Ed2lover, Edcolins, EdgeOfEpsilon, Edgeware, Editorguy007, Edward, Eeekster, Egonitron, Ehlkej, Ehrenkater, EivindJ, Ejnogarb, Elcobbola, ElinorD, Eliz81, Elliotharmon, Elvey, Emana, Enviroboy, Epbr123, Eran of Arcadia, Escape Orbit, Eubulides, Evil Monkey, Ewquillian, Explicit, Faradayplank, FatalError, Felixpace, Ferkelparade, Feseg, Fieldday-sunday, FinalRapture, Financenet, Finngall, Flagman7, FlameintheFog, Flawiki, Flewis, Flowanda, Fly by Night, Forteblast, Forumwriter, Frecklefoot, Fredrik, FrenchIsAwesome, Frenchgeek, Friday is good, Funke, Furrykef, Fuzheado, Fyyer, Fæ, GBYehuda, GCarty, GDonato, Gabelstaplerfahrer, Gaius Cornelius, Garybrimley, Gcapp1959, GeneralBelly, Gerrit, GirlForLife, Glen, Glennmate, Golbez, Gracenotes, GraemeL, Graibeard, GreenReaper, Greenbough, Greensburger, Gregalton, Ground, Ground Zero, Guelly, Gurch, Gurchzilla, Guroadrunner, Gwernol, Gyrobo, Hadal, HaeB, Happyyoyoyo17, Harryzilber, Hbquikcomjamesl, Hdt83, Heimstern, Hellennko, Hellno2, Hennessey, Patrick, Heron, Hirak 99, HisSpaceResearch, Hmains, Hokie92, Hornplease, Hotsaucedude, Howard nyc, Hu, II MusLiM HyBRiD II, IMSoP, Ian3055, IanManka, Ice, IeuanFTW, Igoldste, Ike9898, Imladenoff, IndustryProj, Inter, Iridescent, IronGargoyle, Itzse, Ixfd64, J.delanoy, JForget, JFreeman, JHunterJ, JLaTondre, Jal, Jamesters, Janke, Jantangring, Jaqui Chapman, Jason spazza, Jasondmath, Jaxhere, Jaydev mukhia, Jaysweet, Jbergquist, Jbubs1975, Jcmorin, Jdelacastro, Jdnac, JeLuF, Jengod, Jerzy, JesseRafe, Jezza starwars, Jiddisch, Jimmy116, Jkeene, JoJan, JoanneB, Jodamn, JoeSmack, Joelm, Johann Wolfgang, John Bennettt, John of Reading, JohnInDC, Johnnsmith2, Johnuniq, Jopemon, Jophus00, JorgeS, Joyous!, Jpers36, Jplimpz, Jraso1, Jrlevine, Jtata, Junglecat, Junkwoman, JustinMc, Juzaily, Jvs.cz, K0k1man, Kasyapa, Kaszeta, Katalaveno, Kbdank71, Kchishol1970, KellyCoinGuy, Keok, Kerotan, Kesuari, Ketsumaru, Khalid hassani, Kiand, Kikumbob, Kilo-Lima, Kimmysharma, King of Hearts, Kingpin13, Kingsweeting, Klackalica, Kmorozov, KnowledgeOfSelf, Knutux, Koavf, Kotiwalo, Kpjas, Kubigula, Kungfuadam, Kuru, Kvasicek, Kvikram, LCD z, LDHan, Lacrimosus, Landon1980, Larry nyc, Larrychiang, Leeatcookerly, LennartBolks, Lerdsuwa, Les boys, Leszek Jańczuk, Leuko, LeyteWolfer, Lightmouse, Lil mikei 214, Lildancergal94, Ling.Nut, Linkspamremover, LittleMatchGirl, Livefeeordie, Localh77, Loewenstein, Logantorres, LogicalSecurity, Londonrome, Loren.wilton, Loudon clear, Lovely Chris, LovesMacs, Lradrama, Ltullo53, Ltullo553, Luna Santin, MBK004, MER-C, MKoltnow, MONGO, Madcoverboy, Madrone, Magicker71, Magioladitis, Mailer diablo, Majorly, Malikbek, Maraton, Marfotic, Marianna1407, Martarius, Martin451, Mateo SA, Mathez9, Matijap, MattieTK, Maurreen, Max Naylor, Maximaximax, Maximilian Schönherr, Maximus Rex, Maxis ftw, Maybaby76, Mbarra, McDogm, Mcdoogenator, Mcraejs, Meelar, Mentifisto, Metasquares, Metrofeed, Mets501, Mic, Michael Dorosh, Michael Essmeyer, Michael Snow, Michael miceli, MichaelDolen, MikeFischer, MikeyTMNT, Mikiemike, Miltonkeynes, Minesweeper, Miquonranger03, Misterx2000, Mitch Ames, Mlpearc, Modular, Moggie2002, Monkeyman, Moondyne, Mordidas, Morning277, Mpalma11, Mr Minchin, MrBucket, MrKG, Mrjinx, Muchness, Multidox, Mwilso24, Mydogategodshat, Mykolas OK, NFH, NYCJosh, Nabla, Naif, Natalie Erin, Natkeeran, Navyfrank67, NawlinWiki, Nbarth, Neep, Netkinetic, Netsnipe, Neverquick, NewEnglandYankee, Newone, Newport Beach, Nhajivandi, Nicklanners, Nicolas M. Perrault, NigelR, Nik42, Ninel, Nirvana2013, Nivix, Njjh201, Nlu, Noddycr, Noswadmot, Notinasnaid, Novusuna, Nposs, Nurg, Nuttycoconut, O1ive, Obli, ObtuseAngle, Odedr, Ohnoitsjamie, Oliviapilip, Omicronpersei8, Omphaloscope, Omrandsu, OneWorld22, Ooblick, Orange Suede Sofa, Orangemike, Oskilian, Ospalh, OverlordQ, Oxling, Oxymoron83, Page2, Pakaran, Paleolith, Pascal666, Paukrus, Paul August, Pavel Vozenilek, Pcbene, Pclover, Pdw44wiki, Pearrari, Peidyen, Pepsicola06, PeteVerdon, Peter Delmonte, Peter Horn, Pgecaj, Pgk, Phil Bordelon, Philip Trueman, Pierre Durand, Pinnerpsk, Pissface, Pizza Puzzle, Pleasantville, Pne, Pnm, Poiuyt Man, Pol098, Prashanthns, President Rhapsody, ProhibitOnions, Prolog, Pschwiesow, Psiphiorg, Pyrope, Qwfp, Qwghlm, Qxz, RB972, RainbowCrane, Ralphybaby, RandomStringOfCharacters, Rangi42, Rd232, Realm of Shadows, RedHillian, Redlining2, Reinderien, RepliCarter, RetiredWikipedian789, Rettetast, RexNL, Rfc1394, Rharun, Rhobite, Ribeyed, Rich Farmbrough, Richard Arthur Norton (1958-), RickK, Rigadoun, Rimshot, Rivalarrival, Rj, Roadrunner, Rob Ward, Robek, Robert Merkel, RobertandKathy, Robidy, Roivas, Romainz, Romeotango, Rory096, Rrburke, Rtcpenguin, RuDeDoGg, Rufus843, Rumping, Rwgardencity, Rxc, Rxtreme, SDC, ST47, Saaga, Saintamh, Salgueiro, Salvar, Sam Barsoom, Samnesral, Sampi, Sanjiv swarup, Saros136, Savcash, Sc3499a, Sc3821, SchfiftyThree, Schissel, Schmelly, Schnazola, SchnitzelMannGreek, SchuminWeb, Schutz, Scott Sanchez, ScottyScotts, Scriberius, Sean Smith, Search4Lancer, Searchme, Secretlondon, Seldumonde, Semperf, Serlin, Shadow1, Shadowjams, Shahab6, Shandm123, Shanes, Shantavira, ShawnVW, Sheprd, Sifaka, Signalhead, Silivrenion, SimonP, Sjakkalle, Sjl, SkiBumMSP, Slasher600, Smalljim, Smallman12q, Smiker, Smyth, Solesuppliers, Sonnevillej, Sophia685, Sottolacqua, Sounder rs, South Bay, SpaceFlight89, Spamguy, SparrowsWing, Spectrumps, Splash, Srose, Srushe, Startstop123, StaticGull, Stay cool, Strait, Stratocracy, Suffusion of Yellow, Sulfis, SunCreator, Sunny alenze, Super-Magician, Susanna, Suzannack, T3h 1337 b0y, TaborL, Tangotango, Tantonb, TaviRider, Tawker, Taxman, Tdstom, Technopat, Teds399, TenOfAllTrades, Tetraedycal, Texture, That Guy, From That Show!, The Anome, The Thing That Should Not Be, ThePointblank, Themortgagechampion, Therealhazel, Theslyrussian, Thesmatestguy, Thingg, Thomas Larsen, Tide rolls, Timrollpickering, Timwikiman, Tnetzel, TomCollins11, Tomelgar, Tommy, Tommy2010, Tonyfaull, Topgun9, Torbjorn, Traxs7, Trusilver, Trysha, Tyrel, U7a, UkPaolo, Ulric1313, Uncle Dick, UncleDouggie, UninvitedCompany, Unknownj, UrsaFoot, User27091, Utcursch, Vaheterdu, Veinor, Versageek, Versus22, Vex5, VictorianMutant, Vindi293, Vishenda, Vojta, Vrenator, Vssun, Vuo, WAvegetarian, WPArgentarius, WWC, Wafulz, Waprap, Waterjuice, Wavelength, WayneLVN, Web-Crawling Stickler, Wereon, Wexcan, Where, Whodatpat, Wiki alf, WikiDriver, Wikianon, Wikieditor06, Wikilibrarian, Wikiphile, Wildyoda, William.alvarez, Wimt, Woemlavy, Woohookitty, Wooster, Work permit, Woseph, Wsanders, Xoloz, Xrecar, Xrt, Yamakiri, Yashgaroth, Ygreenman, Yintan, Yourmanstan, Yummifruitbat, Yupik, ZX81, Zachlipton, Zaian, Zalgo, Zanimum, Zarsh, Zelchenko, Zepheus, Zhoutong, Ziusudra, Zzuuzz, מראהנייר ירעל, 1969 anonymous edits

Investment *Source*: http://en.wikipedia.org/w/index.php?title=Investment *Contributors*: -oo0(GoldTrader)0oo-, 5464536, 72Dino, 88jim.klein, ARog, Abc518, AdamWalker, Ahoerstemeier, Airconswitch, Airodyssey, Albertod4, Aleahey, Aleksander.adamowski, Aleksd, Alokagga, Alphachimp, Alucard (Dr.), Amenzel, AmosWolfe, Anaxial, Andman8, Andonic, Andres C., AndrewTJ31, Andrewpmk, Andycjp, AngelOfSadness, Antandrus, Antique Rose, Antonmind, Apnakharian, Ask123, Atif.t2, AudiKiskowski, Babybear2, Barek, Basharh, Bcartolo, Beetstra, Bella Swan, Ben5082, Bgsummit, Bigsean0300, BlueAg09, Bonatto, Bongwarrior, Bookinvestor, Booyahhayoob, Borneo point, Bovineone, Bped1985, Brick Thrower, Bsissons, Bsullivan24, Burn, Bwehttam, C628, CCHIPSS, Cadmccall, CambridgeBayWeather, Campoftheamericas, Capricorn42, Carax, Cflm001, Chaojoker, Clear memory, ClementSeveillac, Cntras, Cordless Larry, Corpx, Cpaolini, DDerby, DVD R W, DarkJyn, DeLarge, DeadEyeArrow, Defekt7x, Deltabeignet, Digitat, Diligent Terrier, Dimorsitanos, DionysosProteus, Diovi, Discospinster, DivineInspiration, DocendoDiscimus, Doulos Christos, Dryman, Duoduoduo, E. James Brennan, Eaolson, Edderso, Edward, El C, Elapsed, Eleassar777, Enchanter, Ernie shoemaker, Espoo, Feco, Ferryca, Firien, Flowanda, Fredbauder, FreplySpang, FunAdventure, Funandtrvl, Gary King, Geeteshgadkari, Ghyfawkes, Giftlite, Goraikkonen, GraemeL, Graydonflatt, Gregdingle, Greyhood, Ground Zero, Groupventure, Gsaup, Gwernol, Hadal, Hede2000, Hemanshu, Hermitage, Heron, HiDrNick, Hu12, IpWorld, IronGargoyle, Iroony, Issam1, Istartfires, J.delanoy, JD554, JForget, JHunterJ, JJMcVey, JYolkowski, JaGa, JackLumber, Jake Larsen, Jamesrk, Jdevine, Jenito, Jerryseinfeld, Jesse627, Jgritz, Jim Douglas, Jiy, Jlang, Joseph Solis in Australia, Josh3580, Jovianeye, Joyroy, Jusdafax, Kaihsu, Karlwick, Katieh5584, Kbrose, Keithf, Khalid hassani, Kikos, Knuckles, Kosebamse, Krakfly, Kruglick, Kuru, Lacrimosus, Lambiam, Legis, Leibniz, Lerdsuwa, Levineps, Lex Pecunia, Linkspamremover, Lisagosselin, Livestone, Lohelennuk, Lookus2010, Louchurno, LowtaxNetwork, Lusitana, M-banker-212, MCogez, MER-C, Madchester, Magister Mathematicae, Mamat Rohimat, Mandarax, Mansuetodigital, ManuP, Marek69, Martin451, MatthewTaylor3, Maurreen, Menquist, Mereda, Mf1420, Mic, Miller2, Minatsu, MirDoc, Mnrk, Monkeyman, Mormegil, Mpbjaderson, Mrmanhattanproject, Murpho12, Mydogategodshat, Mymama, N5iln, Nakon, NeilN, Netsnipe, NewEnglandYankee, Nickturton, Nirvana2013, Notinasnaid, Nsaa, NuclearWarfare, Nyvhek, Ohnoitsjamie, Olimpiu stefan, Olivier, Operdyne7, Originnick, Oxymoron83, Pakaran, Paramountpublishing, Parent5446, PaterMcFly, Patrick, Patstuart, Pauly04, Pearrari, Pedro, Pennyday, Pgan002, Pgreenfinch, Philip Baird Shearer, Philip Trueman, Phillyguy002000, Plinkit, Pm master, Pnm, Polyamorph, Poppy, Prashanthns, Prokopenya Viktor, Publicly Visible, REIAlliance, RJASE1, RadioKirk, RainbowOfLight, Randomtime, Ranksubmit, Raul654, Richhoncho, Rinconsoleao, Rkitko, Rob Hooft, Robertgreer, Robykiwi, Romansemko, Rrburke, SL93, SMC, SMcCandlish, Sagsaw, Sammyjmoseley, Sardanaphalus, Satori Son, Savh, Scmbwis, Sendoh, Sewebster, Shadow1, Shadowjams, Shawnc, Sietse Snel, Siim, Sikander7860, Silverbach, Simon123, SimonP, SiobhanHansa, Skarebo, Smallbones, Smallman12q, Smee, Steven Zhang, Stevenmitchell, Stevertigo, Stikemanforum, TastyPoutine, Tawker, Taxman, Texture, The Ent, TheLetterM, Thingg, Thomasmeeks, Thrane, TigerShark, TimShell, Titoxd, Toon05, Trevhowes, Trusilver, Ttmmblogger, Tubby, Twigletmac, Undead warrior, Useight, Uwho, Versageek, Vervin, Vivsaks, Vkem, Walden, Washburnmav, Wavelength, Wayne Slam, Welsh, WereSpielChequers, Why Not A Duck, WikiTikiWiki, Wikipeterproject, Wikiwiki789, Wmahan, Woohookitty, Worlock eats, Xcvxcvsdfdsf42, Xdenizen, Xliamdx, Yuda5148, Zarcadia, Ziva David, Zzuuzz, 569 anonymous edits

Image Sources, Licenses and Contributors

File:Ssfcu logo.png *Source*: http://en.wikipedia.org/w/index.php?title=File:Ssfcu_logo.png *License*: unknown *Contributors*: Gobonobo

File:Credit Union in Warangal, India.JPG *Source*: http://en.wikipedia.org/w/index.php?title=File:Credit_Union_in_Warangal,_India.JPG *License*: unknown *Contributors*: User:Brett epic

File:F.W.Raiffeisen.jpg *Source*: http://en.wikipedia.org/w/index.php?title=File:F.W.Raiffeisen.jpg *License*: unknown *Contributors*: Gobonobo

File:CaissePopulaireShediac.jpg *Source*: http://en.wikipedia.org/w/index.php?title=File:CaissePopulaireShediac.jpg *License*: unknown *Contributors*: Verne Equinox

File:SA Montage Nima.png *Source*: http://en.wikipedia.org/w/index.php?title=File:SA_Montage_Nima.png *License*: unknown *Contributors*: User:Zereshk

File:Flag of San Antonio, Texas.svg *Source*: http://en.wikipedia.org/w/index.php?title=File:Flag_of_San_Antonio,_Texas.svg *License*: unknown *Contributors*: City of San Antonio website

File:Sanantonioseal.jpeg *Source*: http://en.wikipedia.org/w/index.php?title=File:Sanantonioseal.jpeg *License*: unknown *Contributors*: Brownings, Jpwashere

File:Bexar SanAntonio.svg *Source*: http://en.wikipedia.org/w/index.php?title=File:Bexar_SanAntonio.svg *License*: unknown *Contributors*: User:25or6to4

file:Usa edcp location map.svg *Source*: http://en.wikipedia.org/w/index.php?title=File:Usa_edcp_location_map.svg *License*: unknown *Contributors*: User:Uwe Dedering

File:Red pog.svg *Source*: http://en.wikipedia.org/w/index.php?title=File:Red_pog.svg *License*: unknown *Contributors*: Anomie

File:Loudspeaker.svg *Source*: http://en.wikipedia.org/w/index.php?title=File:Loudspeaker.svg *License*: unknown *Contributors*: Bayo, Gmaxwell, Husky, Iamunknown, Myself488, Nethac DIU, Omegatron, Rocket000, The Evil IP address, Wouterhagens, 11 anonymous edits

File:San Antonio, Texas in 1886.jpg *Source*: http://en.wikipedia.org/w/index.php?title=File:San_Antonio,_Texas_in_1886.jpg *License*: unknown *Contributors*: Augustus Koch (1840–?)

File:AlamoMemorial-5478.jpg *Source*: http://en.wikipedia.org/w/index.php?title=File:AlamoMemorial-5478.jpg *License*: unknown *Contributors*: User:Loadmaster

File:San antonio tex 1939.jpg *Source*: http://en.wikipedia.org/w/index.php?title=File:San_antonio_tex_1939.jpg *License*: unknown *Contributors*: Infrogmation, OTAVIO1981, Túrelio, Xnatedawgx

File:STMC SA.jpg *Source*: http://en.wikipedia.org/w/index.php?title=File:STMC_SA.jpg *License*: unknown *Contributors*: Buchanan-Hermit, TexasAndroid, Zereshk, 1 anonymous edits

File:Valero campus (2).JPG *Source*: http://en.wikipedia.org/w/index.php?title=File:Valero_campus_(2).JPG *License*: unknown *Contributors*: User:Zereshk

File:Alamo TX.jpg *Source*: http://en.wikipedia.org/w/index.php?title=File:Alamo_TX.jpg *License*: unknown *Contributors*: Eixo on en.wikipedia

File:Riverwalk Christmas 05-2.jpg *Source*: http://en.wikipedia.org/w/index.php?title=File:Riverwalk_Christmas_05-2.jpg *License*: unknown *Contributors*: User:Zereshk

File:SA Torch of Friendship.JPG *Source*: http://en.wikipedia.org/w/index.php?title=File:SA_Torch_of_Friendship.JPG *License*: unknown *Contributors*: Dknights411, TexasAndroid

File:Rio del pasio 05.jpg *Source*: http://en.wikipedia.org/w/index.php?title=File:Rio_del_pasio_05.jpg *License*: unknown *Contributors*: TexasAndroid, Zereshk

File:SA hotel view.jpg *Source*: http://en.wikipedia.org/w/index.php?title=File:SA_hotel_view.jpg *License*: unknown *Contributors*: User:Zereshk

File:SAPL2.jpg *Source*: http://en.wikipedia.org/w/index.php?title=File:SAPL2.jpg *License*: unknown *Contributors*: User:Zereshk

File:SA SN tree.jpg *Source*: http://en.wikipedia.org/w/index.php?title=File:SA_SN_tree.jpg *License*: unknown *Contributors*: User:Zereshk

File:Bexar County Court House perspective.jpg *Source*: http://en.wikipedia.org/w/index.php?title=File:Bexar_County_Court_House_perspective.jpg *License*: unknown *Contributors*: Nima Kasraie (Zereshk on en.wikipedia)

File:SACC Nima.jpg *Source*: http://en.wikipedia.org/w/index.php?title=File:SACC_Nima.jpg *License*: unknown *Contributors*: User:Zereshk

File:The Shops at La Cantera in San Antonio, TX (outside shot) IMG_1159.JPG *Source*: http://en.wikipedia.org/w/index.php?title=File:The_Shops_at_La_Cantera_in_San_Antonio,_TX_(outside_shot)_IMG_1159.JPG *License*: unknown *Contributors*: User:Billy Hathorn

File:SABG8.jpg *Source*: http://en.wikipedia.org/w/index.php?title=File:SABG8.jpg *License*: unknown *Contributors*: User:Zereshk

File:Mission-Concepcion.jpg *Source*: http://en.wikipedia.org/w/index.php?title=File:Mission-Concepcion.jpg *License*: unknown *Contributors*: Georgeryp, Jareha, Rüdiger Wölk, The Jacobin, Zereshk

File:SeaWorldTexas1.jpg *Source*: http://en.wikipedia.org/w/index.php?title=File:SeaWorldTexas1.jpg *License*: unknown *Contributors*: Hailey C. Shannon, Rei

File:Aztec On The River - Building.jpg *Source*: http://en.wikipedia.org/w/index.php?title=File:Aztec_On_The_River_-_Building.jpg *License*: unknown *Contributors*: Charou, TexasAndroid

File:Fiestatexaslogo.png *Source*: http://en.wikipedia.org/w/index.php?title=File:Fiestatexaslogo.png *License*: unknown *Contributors*: User:66.69.98.29, User:BetacommandBot, User:Brownings, User:Clipper471, User:Cydebot, User:Elipongo, User:Polbot

File:SAIMAX.JPG *Source*: http://en.wikipedia.org/w/index.php?title=File:SAIMAX.JPG *License*: unknown *Contributors*: Justin Hundsnurscher

File:HBGConven.JPG *Source*: http://en.wikipedia.org/w/index.php?title=File:HBGConven.JPG *License*: unknown *Contributors*: Dhdez05

File:ATTCenter.jpg *Source*: http://en.wikipedia.org/w/index.php?title=File:ATTCenter.jpg *License*: unknown *Contributors*: Original uploader was Dknights411 at en.wikipedia

File:UTSAcampus2.jpg *Source*: http://en.wikipedia.org/w/index.php?title=File:UTSAcampus2.jpg *License*: unknown *Contributors*: User:Zereshk

File:San Antonio Intersection.JPG *Source*: http://en.wikipedia.org/w/index.php?title=File:San_Antonio_Intersection.JPG *License*: unknown *Contributors*: Original uploader was Dknights411 at en.wikipedia

File:Woaitvstation.jpg *Source*: http://en.wikipedia.org/w/index.php?title=File:Woaitvstation.jpg *License*: unknown *Contributors*: Brownings, Dknights411, TexasAndroid

File:Flag of Mexico.svg *Source*: http://en.wikipedia.org/w/index.php?title=File:Flag_of_Mexico.svg *License*: unknown *Contributors*: User:AlexCovarrubias

File:Flag of Spain.svg *Source*: http://en.wikipedia.org/w/index.php?title=File:Flag_of_Spain.svg *License*: unknown *Contributors*: Anomie

File:Flag of South Korea.svg *Source*: http://en.wikipedia.org/w/index.php?title=File:Flag_of_South_Korea.svg *License*: unknown *Contributors*: Various

File:Flag of the Republic of China.svg *Source*: http://en.wikipedia.org/w/index.php?title=File:Flag_of_the_Republic_of_China.svg *License*: unknown *Contributors*: 555, Bestalex, Bigmorr, Denelson83, Ed veg, Gzdavidwong, Herbythyme, Isletakee, Kakoui, Kallerna, Kibinsky, Mattes, Mizunoryu, Neq00, Nickpo, Nightstallion, Odder, Pymouss, R.O.C, Reisio, Reuvenk, Rkt2312, Rocket000, Runningfridgesrule, Samwingkit, Sasha Krotov, Shizhao, Tabasco, Vzb83, Wrightbus, ZooFari, Zscout370, 72 anonymous edits

File:Flag of Japan.svg *Source*: http://en.wikipedia.org/w/index.php?title=File:Flag_of_Japan.svg *License*: unknown *Contributors*: Anomie

File:Flag of India.svg *Source*: http://en.wikipedia.org/w/index.php?title=File:Flag_of_India.svg *License*: unknown *Contributors*: Anomie, Mifter

File:Flag of the People's Republic of China.svg *Source*: http://en.wikipedia.org/w/index.php?title=File:Flag_of_the_People's_Republic_of_China.svg *License*: unknown *Contributors*: User:Denelson83, User:SKopp, User:Shizhao, User:Zscout370

File:Flag of Germany.svg *Source*: http://en.wikipedia.org/w/index.php?title=File:Flag_of_Germany.svg *License*: unknown *Contributors*: Anomie

File:Flag of Israel.svg *Source*: http://en.wikipedia.org/w/index.php?title=File:Flag_of_Israel.svg *License*: unknown *Contributors*: AnonMoos, Bastique, Bobika, Brown spite, Captain Zizi, Cerveaugenie, Drork, Etams, Fred J, Fry1989, Geagea, Himasaram, Homo lupus, Humus sapiens, Klemen Kocjancic, Kookaburra, Luispihormiguero, Madden, Neq00, NielsF, Nightstallion, Oren neu dag, Patstuart, PeeJay2K3, Pumbaa80, Ramiy, Reisio, SKopp, Sceptic, SomeDudeWithAUserName, Technion, Typhix, Valentinian, Yellow up, Zscout370, 31 anonymous edits

File:Downtown-san-antonio.jpeg *Source*: http://en.wikipedia.org/w/index.php?title=File:Downtown-san-antonio.jpeg *License*: unknown *Contributors*: P.o.h, Wames, Xnatedawgx, Zereshk

Image:CorpusChristiTX Night.jpg *Source*: http://en.wikipedia.org/w/index.php?title=File:CorpusChristiTX_Night.jpg *License*: unknown *Contributors*: Xnatedawgx, Yassie

Image:San Agustin Cathedral.JPG *Source*: http://en.wikipedia.org/w/index.php?title=File:San_Agustin_Cathedral.JPG *License*: unknown *Contributors*: User:AMAPO

File:Brnelizand10thst.jpg *Source*: http://en.wikipedia.org/w/index.php?title=File:Brnelizand10thst.jpg *License*: unknown *Contributors*: Original uploader was Jaedza at en.wikipedia

File:Mcallen.jpg *Source*: http://en.wikipedia.org/w/index.php?title=File:Mcallen.jpg *License*: unknown *Contributors*: Rgv17_956

Image:Padre Island National Seashore - sand dunes3.jpg *Source*: http://en.wikipedia.org/w/index.php?title=File:Padre_Island_National_Seashore_-_sand_dunes3.jpg *License*: unknown *Contributors*: User:Johntex

Image:Regions of Texas.PNG *Source*: http://en.wikipedia.org/w/index.php?title=File:Regions_of_Texas.PNG *License*: unknown *Contributors*: Atownballer (talk) Original uploader was Atownballer at en.wikipedia

Image:I-10.svg *Source*: http://en.wikipedia.org/w/index.php?title=File:I-10.svg *License*: unknown *Contributors*: Augiasstallputzer, Infrogmation, Juliancolton, Ltljltlj, Rocket000, SPUI, 1 anonymous edits

Image:I-35.svg *Source*: http://en.wikipedia.org/w/index.php?title=File:I-35.svg *License*: unknown *Contributors*: 1coolkid, Augiasstallputzer, Bidgee, Faiyazamzad, Fran Rogers, InterstateKazuya40, Kazuya35, Ltljltlj, SPUI, T2, Xnatedawgx, 1 anonymous edits

Image:I-37.svg *Source*: http://en.wikipedia.org/w/index.php?title=File:I-37.svg *License*: unknown *Contributors*: Augiasstallputzer, Ltljltlj, SPUI, Xnatedawgx, 1 anonymous edits

Image:I-69.svg *Source*: http://en.wikipedia.org/w/index.php?title=File:I-69.svg *License*: unknown *Contributors*: Augiasstallputzer, Ltljltlj, Rocket000, SPUI

Image:US 59.svg *Source*: http://en.wikipedia.org/w/index.php?title=File:US_59.svg *License*: unknown *Contributors*: Bidgee, Infrogmation, SPUI, Xnatedawgx, 3 anonymous edits

Image:US 77.svg *Source*: http://en.wikipedia.org/w/index.php?title=File:US_77.svg *License*: unknown *Contributors*: Bidgee, SPUI, Xnatedawgx, 2 anonymous edits

Image:US 83.svg *Source*: http://en.wikipedia.org/w/index.php?title=File:US_83.svg *License*: unknown *Contributors*: Bidgee, SPUI, Xnatedawgx, 2 anonymous edits

Image:US 87.svg *Source*: http://en.wikipedia.org/w/index.php?title=File:US_87.svg *License*: unknown *Contributors*: Bidgee, SPUI, Xnatedawgx, 3 anonymous edits

Image:US 181.svg *Source*: http://en.wikipedia.org/w/index.php?title=File:US_181.svg *License*: unknown *Contributors*: Common Good, SPUI

Image:US 281.svg *Source*: http://en.wikipedia.org/w/index.php?title=File:US_281.svg *License*: unknown *Contributors*: SPUI, Xnatedawgx

Image:Texas 4.svg *Source*: http://en.wikipedia.org/w/index.php?title=File:Texas_4.svg *License*: unknown *Contributors*: Rocket000, SPUI

Image:Texas 16.svg *Source*: http://en.wikipedia.org/w/index.php?title=File:Texas_16.svg *License*: unknown *Contributors*: SPUI

Image:Texas 44.svg *Source*: http://en.wikipedia.org/w/index.php?title=File:Texas_44.svg *License*: unknown *Contributors*: SPUI

Image:Texas 107.svg *Source*: http://en.wikipedia.org/w/index.php?title=File:Texas_107.svg *License*: unknown *Contributors*: SPUI

Image:Toll Texas 255.svg *Source*: http://en.wikipedia.org/w/index.php?title=File:Toll_Texas_255.svg *License*: unknown *Contributors*: Holderca1

Image:Texas 336.svg *Source*: http://en.wikipedia.org/w/index.php?title=File:Texas_336.svg *License*: unknown *Contributors*: Holderca1

Image:Texas 359.svg *Source*: http://en.wikipedia.org/w/index.php?title=File:Texas_359.svg *License*: unknown *Contributors*: Holderca1

Image:Texas 361.svg *Source*: http://en.wikipedia.org/w/index.php?title=File:Texas_361.svg *License*: unknown *Contributors*: Holderca1

Image:Texas 495.svg *Source*: http://en.wikipedia.org/w/index.php?title=File:Texas_495.svg *License*: unknown *Contributors*: Holderca1

Image:Texas 141.svg *Source*: http://en.wikipedia.org/w/index.php?title=File:Texas_141.svg *License*: unknown *Contributors*: SPUI

Image:Texas 285.svg *Source*: http://en.wikipedia.org/w/index.php?title=File:Texas_285.svg *License*: unknown *Contributors*: SPUI

Image:SanAntonio-RiverWalk-5160.jpg *Source*: http://en.wikipedia.org/w/index.php?title=File:SanAntonio-RiverWalk-5160.jpg *License*: unknown *Contributors*: User:Loadmaster

Image:South Padre Island beach.jpg *Source*: http://en.wikipedia.org/w/index.php?title=File:South_Padre_Island_beach.jpg *License*: unknown *Contributors*: Original uploader was Brendajane at en.wikipedia

Image:SeaWorldTexas1.jpg *Source*: http://en.wikipedia.org/w/index.php?title=File:SeaWorldTexas1.jpg *License*: unknown *Contributors*: Hailey C. Shannon, Rei

Image:Mission San Antonio aka Alamo.jpg *Source*: http://en.wikipedia.org/w/index.php?title=File:Mission_San_Antonio_aka_Alamo.jpg *License*: unknown *Contributors*: moi

Image:December_20_-_Corpus_-_003.jpg *Source*: http://en.wikipedia.org/w/index.php?title=File:December_20_-_Corpus_-_003.jpg *License*: unknown *Contributors*: User:Atownballer

File:USS Lexington Corpus.JPG *Source*: http://en.wikipedia.org/w/index.php?title=File:USS_Lexington_Corpus.JPG *License*: unknown *Contributors*: User:Liveon001

File:San Agustin Cathedral Tower.JPG *Source*: http://en.wikipedia.org/w/index.php?title=File:San_Agustin_Cathedral_Tower.JPG *License*: unknown *Contributors*: User:AMAPO

File:Rio Grande Republic Capitol.jpg *Source*: http://en.wikipedia.org/w/index.php?title=File:Rio_Grande_Republic_Capitol.jpg *License*: unknown *Contributors*: User:AMAPO

Image:SampleBankbook.png *Source*: http://en.wikipedia.org/w/index.php?title=File:SampleBankbook.png *License*: unknown *Contributors*: w:User:AirodysseySergio Ortega

Image:CanadianChequeSample.png *Source*: http://en.wikipedia.org/w/index.php?title=File:CanadianChequeSample.png *License*: unknown *Contributors*: Original uploader was Airodyssey at en.wikipedia

Image:ATM 750x1300.jpg *Source*: http://en.wikipedia.org/w/index.php?title=File:ATM_750x1300.jpg *License*: unknown *Contributors*: Original uploader was Rfc1394 at en.wikipedia Later versions were uploaded by Awyong Jeffrey Mordecai Salleh at en.wikipedia.

File:Mortgage-Rates-Historical.png *Source*: http://en.wikipedia.org/w/index.php?title=File:Mortgage-Rates-Historical.png *License*: unknown *Contributors*: User:Canadarates

File:Smartcard2.png *Source*: http://en.wikipedia.org/w/index.php?title=File:Smartcard2.png *License*: unknown *Contributors*: User:Channel R

File:Creditcardwcontactless.png *Source*: http://en.wikipedia.org/w/index.php?title=File:Creditcardwcontactless.png *License*: unknown *Contributors*: User:Chairsenses

File:CCardBack.svg *Source*: http://en.wikipedia.org/w/index.php?title=File:CCardBack.svg *License*: unknown *Contributors*: Alexander Jones

File:WeTakeCreditDebitCardsCrop.jpg *Source*: http://en.wikipedia.org/w/index.php?title=File:WeTakeCreditDebitCardsCrop.jpg *License*: unknown *Contributors*: Neep, 1 anonymous edits

File:Smartcard3.png *Source*: http://en.wikipedia.org/w/index.php?title=File:Smartcard3.png *License*: unknown *Contributors*: User:Channel R

FSC
www.fsc.org
MIX
Papier | Fördert gute Waldnutzung
FSC® C083411

Kolibri 360 GmbH
Ferdinand-Jühlke-Straße 7
99095 Erfurt, Deutschland
produktsicherheit@kolibri360.de

Druck:
CPI Druckdienstleistungen GmbH
im Auftrag der
Kolibri 360 GmbH
Ferdinand-Jühlke-Str. 7
99095 Erfurt